A Gardener's Compendium

GARDENING IN A TWITTER WORLD
IN 140 CHARACTERS OR MORE

Volume 3

GARDENING WITH THE SENSES

TERESA WATKINS

XULON PRESS

Xulon Press
2301 Lucien Way #415
Maitland, FL 32751
407.339.4217
www.xulonpress.com

Printed in the United States of America.

Paperback ISBN-13: 978-1-6628-0536-3
eBook ISBN-13: 978-1-6628-0537-0

Dedicated to my grandchildren,

Jaxon, Mackenah, Xavier, Madison, Katlyn,

Raegan, Bella, Emma, Katarina, Kadence,

and Olivia.

Other Books by Teresa Watkins

"A Gardener's Compendium"
Volume 1 – Gardening with Life

"A Gardener's Compendium"
Volume 2 – Gardening in Time and Place"

We write to make sense of it all.

Wallace Stegner (1909 – 1993)
American novelist, environmentalist
On Teaching and Writing Fiction (2002)
Paraphrasing John Cheever *(2019)*[1]
#books #writing #UnitedStates

Be sure that you go to the author to get at his meaning, not to find yours.

John Ruskin (1819 – 1900)
English art critic
'Of Kings' Treasuries'
Sesame and Lilies (1865)
#author #books #England #literature #novel

---

[1] Source: Verified by Lynda Stegner (2019)

The greatest gift of the garden is the restoration of the five senses.

Hanna Rion Ver Beck (1875 – 1924)
English painter and children books' illustrator
Let's Make A Flower Garden (1912)
#England #health #rejuvenation

There are strange flowers of reason to match each error of the senses.

Louis Aragon (1897 – 1982)
French editor, novelist, poet
Paris Peasant (1926)

#France #reason

ACKNOWLEDGEMENTS

My senses are overflowing with gratitude on the publishing of *A Gardener's Compendium Volume 3 – Gardening with the Senses (#AGC)*. It was almost lost forever to a series of unfortunate life events. I would like to thank the following persons for their timely help and support in my writing and research:

To Malcolm Jamieson, of DTIData for recovering the entire draft of AGC from a crashed hard drive four years later. Without your help, Volume 3 or the following AGC volumes of the series would not be published.

As *Volume 3 – Gardening with the Senses* comprises "Gardening with the Physic," it's my opportunity to thank Dr. Jeffrey Greenwald, Dr. Jonathan Zager, Dr. Richard Bosshardt, and the nurses and techs of Moffitt Cancer Center. Each of you made critical decisions that saved my life.

Thank you to Joseph Hayes, writer, playwright, supporter of the arts, for his generosity of spirit to a complete stranger. Joel took the time to honestly help define my desires, encourage me to write all my book ideas, and to write *A Gardener's Compendium* in a series of volumes.

Thank you to Annie Hooper for your prayers, support, and belief in family over the years. I can't tell you how much you are loved.

` I was able to finish the book and get it published in time so that my Dad, Stoffel Jack Burton, could see it before he died. Working with him in two businesses in different industries, our careers paralleled each other in so many ways. I am grateful for what he taught me. I can never thank you enough, Dad, for all of your love, support, and life events that you allowed me to experience with you..

To my husband, Tony, my best friend, the love of my life, and my cornerstone, thank you for everything you do for me and our family.

Teresa Watkins

SHE CONSULTING

INTRODUCTION

When I was a little girl, our swing set was in a huge wooden sandbox in the backyard. What fun we — my five siblings and I — had digging holes, filling up buckets, and playing in the white sand, making pies with our hands. The joy that comes from digging in the ground never leaves you. Today, science research (Lowry, 2007) explains why children are so happy digging in the dirt. Microbes in dirt enhance serotonin levels and makes children feel better. As adults, gardening increases our "happy" pheromones. Despite the length of time (whether a leisurely 15 minutes or a dawn-to-dusk project), sweat investment, or intensity of hard work, whether we pull a few weeds, plant flowers, or spend hours clearing ground for next season's crops, we feel good when we dig in the dirt. Digging for and collecting garden quotes, anecdotes, and stories makes me happy. *A Gardener's Compendium – Gardening in a Twitter World in a 140 Characters or More* (AGC) is my seven (perhaps eight?)

volume series of my passion and/or obsession to know the five W's: who, what, when where, and why. Who wrote that? What is it about? Where did it take place? When was that said? Why does this quote have attributions to three different people? As a garden communicator and researcher, I have found Internet and Facebook posts, website gardening phrases, blogs posting a tweet or quote without attribution to be frustrating. As an example, in this volume, there is the quote *"Gardening requires lots of water — most of it in the form of perspiration."* It appears copiously in 40-year old newspapers, blogs, social media, and world-wide websites citing Lou Erickson as the author. Most of these sites do not mention which Lou Erickson, just "Lou Erickson." Others credit a specific Lou Erickson. Is it Lou (Louise) Erickson (1929 – 2016), the female pitcher who played from 1948 through 1950 in the All-American Girls Professional Baseball League, featured in *A League of Their Own* (1992)? Or is it Lou (Louise) Erickson (1928 – 2019), the famous Hollywood actress known as the star of "Rosie the Riveter" (1944)? Finally, there is Lou Bernard Erickson (1913 – 1990), the talented *Atlanta Journal* editorial illustrator and cartoonist. All three persons have been quoted on the World Wide Web as the original source of this wonderfully sweaty gardening quote. After many years of research, I think I have deduced who said it based on reasonable facts.

In researching Louise Erickson, nicknamed Lou by her baseball team, she may have planted flowers in her lifetime, but there is no proof that she was quoted or even thought of sweating from anything but playing baseball. She's out! I couldn't find Lou Erickson, the movie actress, discussing flowers or gardening at all, but Lou Bernard Erickson, the prolific editorial cartoonist and genius behind "Lou's Notes", did pen his personal quips every week. His twenty-plus-years weekly newspaper column in *The Atlanta Journal* was a popular feature that had Lou's one to three-liner thoughts on everything from 20th century politics, weather, culture, to life events. Despite wonderful assistance from Sandi West, *The Atlanta Journal-Constitution* News Information Specialist, we couldn't find the newspapers for every week *The*

Atlanta Journal was published. So, while never actually sourcing the original date, I am 99% confident that Lou Erickson, of "Lou's Notes" fame is the original source. What do you think?

(AGC) *Volume 3—Gardening with the Senses* chapters encompass the five recognized senses humanity possesses, along with common sense and the sense of well-being: health. You will find every inclusion with full attributions possible along with the original date, grammar, spelling, and my other floral obsession: botanical points for horticultural name. The obvious hashtags -- #gardening, #hearing, #scent, #sight, #smell, #sound, #touch, #commonsense, and #senses -- are implied or you can create your own. As always, in finding and sourcing my volumes, I personally learned more going through and proving my sources that I find useful, fascinating, and fun. I hope you enjoy "A Gardener's Compendium Volume 3's Gardening with the Senses" collection and that you *feel* better after reading and your senses are enhanced when gardening.

Garden with your soul,

Teresa W Watkins

SHE CONSULTING

GARDENING WITH SCENT

'I ought not to have listened to her,' he confided to me one day. 'One never ought to listen to the flowers. One should simply look at them and breathe their fragrance. Mine perfumed all my planet. But I did not know how to take pleasure in all her grace.'

Antoine de Saint-Exupéry (1900 – 1944)

French aristocrat, writer, poet, and pioneering aviator

The Little Prince (1943)

#France #fragrance #literature #perfume

Scents bring memories, and many memories bring nostalgic pleasure. We would be wise to plan for this when we plant a garden.

Thalassa Cruso (1909 – 1997)
English garden writer, celebrity horticulturist
To Everything There Is a Season: The Gardening Year (1973)
#design #England #landscape #memories

Here kindly warmth their mounting juice ferments

To nobler tastes, and more exalted scents:

E'en the rough rocks with tender myrtle bloom, and trodden weeds

send out a rich perfume.

Joseph Addison (1672 – 1719)
English essayist, poet, playwright, and politician
A Letter From Italy (1709)
"To The Right Honourable Charles Lord Halifax
In The Year MDCCI" (1703)
#England #foreign #Italy #perfume #poetry #tours #travel

Salt is added to dried rose petals with the perfume and spices, when we store them away in covered jars, the summers of our past.

Wallace Stegner (1909 – 1993)
American novelist, environmentalist, historian
Angle of Repose (1971)
#history #literature #perfume #potpourri #spices #Summer #UnitedStates

The breath of flowers is far sweeter in the air (where it comes and goes like the warbling of music) than in the hand.[2]

Sir Francis Bacon (1561–1626)
English philosopher, statesman, scientist, essayist, author
"Of Gardens" (1625)
The Essayes or Counsels, Civills and Moralls, of Francis Lo.
Veralum Viscount St. Alban (1625)[3]
#air #design #England #essays #music #wind

---

[2] Paraphrased by George William Curtis: "The fragrance always stays in the hand that gives the rose."

[3] For entire essay, see Watkins, Teresa, *A Gardener's Compendium – Gardening in Time and Place, Vol 2,* Xulon Press, 2017.

I drank in fragrance a thousand times more sweet than a hyacinth's lip.

Barry Waller Procter (pseud. Cornwall) (1784 – 1787)
English poet
*Dramatic Scenes: and other poems (*1819**)**
#England #poetry #sweetness

It was a fruit without flavor, a flower without fragrance, a symphony without melody, a dinner without speeches.

George William Curtis (1824– 1892)
American journalist, editor, public speaker
Literary and Social Essays of George Wm. Curtis (1895)
#culture #essays #fruit #literature #politics #UnitedStates

When the Persian Poet Hafiz was asked by the Philosopher Zenda what he was good for, he replied:
"Of what use is a flower?"
"A flower is good to smell," said the philosopher.
"And I am good to smell it," said the poet.

Persian traditional legend
George William Curtis (1824– 1892)
American journalist, editor, public speaker
Nile notes of a Howadji (1852)
#Iran #Persia #philosophy #purpose #UnitedStates

The beautiful isolation of the rose in its own fragrance is self–sufficient.

George William Curtis (1824– 1892)
American journalist, editor, public speaker
Early Letters of George Wm. Curtis to John S. Dwight (1898)
#sufficiency #UnitedStates

A porcupine hides his flesh in bristling quills; but a magnolia, when its time has not yet come, folds its heart in and in with over–lacing tissues of creamy richness and fragrance. The flower is not sullen, it is only secret.

George William Curtis (1824– 1892)
American journalist, editor, public speaker
Trumps (1861)
#protection #secret # #wildlife #UnitedStates

A young person, with a beautiful face and of a higher origin, however, uneducated is always ignored like a scentless flower.

Chanakya (370 BC – 283 BC)
Indian teacher, philosopher, economist.
Chanakya Niti (3rd BC – 2nd BC)
#beauty #education #India #philosophy #proverbs

I had stopped my chair at that exact place, coming out, because right there the spice of wisteria that hung around the house was invaded by the freshness of apple blossoms in a blend that lift the top of my head. As between those who notice such things and those who don't, I prefer those who do.

Wallace Stegner (1909 – 1993)
American novelist, environmentalist, historian
Angle of Repose (1971)
#fruit #landscape #literature #spices #UnitedStates

Ah, County Guy, the hour is nigh,

The sun has left the lea.

The orange flower perfumes the bower,

The breeze is on the sea.

Sir Walter Scott (1771 – 1832)
Scottish historical novelist, poet, playwright, historian
Quentin Durward (1823)
#literature #novel #perfume #poetry #Scotland #wind

It's so nice to get flowers while you can still smell the fragrance.

Lena Horne (1917 – 2010)
American singer, dancer, actress, and civil rights activist
<u>People</u> magazine (November 10, 1980)
#celebrity #gifts #Hollywood #UnitedStates

'Tis not the fairest form that holds

The mildest, purest soul within;

'Tis not the richest plant that holds

The sweetest fragrance in.

Rufus Dawes (1803 – 1859)
American businessman, Congressman, and author
"To Cressida"
The Valley of The Nashaway and other poems (1830)
#goodness #poetry #UnitedStates #wealth

People often... have no idea how fair the flower is to the touch, nor
do they appreciate its fragrance, which is the soul of the flower.

Helen Keller (1880 – 1868)
American author, political activist, lecturer
To Love This Life: Quotations by Helen Keller (2000)
#beauty #delight #soul #UnitedStates

I believe that God is in me as the sun is in the color and fragrance

of a flower—the Light in my darkness, the Voice in my silence.

Helen Keller (1880 – 1868)
American author, political activist, lecturer
Midstream My Later Life (1930)
#beauty #delight #God #UnitedStates

Not a flower

But shows some touch, in freckle, streak or stain,

Of his unrivall'd pencil. He inspires

Their balmy odors, and imparts their hues,

And bathes their eyes with nectar, and includes

In grains as countless as the seaside sands,

The forms with which he sprinkles all the earth

Happy who walks with him!

William Cowper (1731 – 1800)
English poet and hymnodist
The Task (1785)
#England #color #poetry #sea #walking

As there are some flowers which you should smell but slightly to extract all that is pleasant in them, and which, if you do otherwise, emit what is unpleasant and noxious, so there are some men with whom a slight acquaintance is quite sufficient to draw out all that is agreeable; a more intimate one would be unsatisfactory and unsafe.

Walter Savage Landor (1775 – 1864)
English writer, poet, and activist
The Works of Walter Savage Landor (1846)
#England #men #noxious #unpleasant

It is a golden maxim to cultivate the garden for the nose, and the eyes will take care of themselves. Nor must the ear be forgotten: without birds, a garden is a prison–yard.

Robert Louis Stevenson (1844 – 1894)
Scottish novelist, travel writer
The Ideal House (1898)[4]
#birds #design #maxims #prison #Scotland

---

[4] *The Ideal House* was an unfinished essay found after Stevenson's death.

Just like a tree laden with scented flowers spreads fragrance in the whole forest. Similarly, a worthy son brings glory to the whole family, community, and the country.

Chanakya (370 BC – 283 BC)
Indian teacher, philosopher, economist
Chanakya Niti (3rd BC – 2nd BC)
#beauty #education #India #philosophy #proverbs

The fragrance of flowers spreads only in the direction of the wind. But the goodness of a person spreads in all directions.

Chanakya (370 BC – 283 BC)[5]
Indian teacher, philosopher, economist
Chanakya Niti (3rd BC – 2nd BC)
#India #goodness #philosophy #proverbs

I think I am quite wicked with roses. I like to gather them, and smell them till they have no scent left.

George Eliot (1819 – 1880)[6]
English novelist, poet, journalist
The Mill on the Floss (1860)
#England #thought #insight

---

[5] Traditionally known as Kauṭilya or Vishnugupta.
[6] Pseudonym of Mary Ann Evans Cross.

Beauty, without virtue, is like a flower without perfume.

Traditional French proverb

Compiled by Adam Woolever (1833 – 1882)

Treasury of Wisdom, Wit and Humor,

Odd Comparisons and Proverbs (1877)

#beauty #perfume #proverbs #virtue #UnitedStates

Found also:

Beauty without virtue is like a rose without scent.

Traditional Swedish proverb

#beauty #proverbs #Sweden

Beauty is an exquisite flower, and its perfume is virtue.[7]

John Hood (1838 – unknown)

American doctor, author, lay theologian

The Beauty of God… (1908)

#beauty #perfume #proverbs #UnitedStates #virtue

---

[7] Also attributed to Giovanni Ruffini (1807-1881) but no source in any of his works.

Mr. Allnut: I'm sorry I gave you such a turn.

Rose: That's quite all right, Mr. Allnut.

Mr. Allnut: Good night, miss.

Rose: Good night, Mr. Allnut.

Rose: What a frightfully strong smell.

Mr. Allnut: What smell?

Rose: The river. It smells like marigolds. Stale ones.

Mr. Allnut: It does, huh?

Rose: Not a very good smell for a flower. They're very pretty, though, marigolds.

Mr. Allnut: They are, huh?

Charlie Allnut (Humphrey Bogart)

Rose[8] Sayer (Katherine Hepburn)

John Huston (1906 – 1987)

American director, United Artists

"The African Queen" (1951)

C. S. Forester (1899 – 1966) [9]

English author

The African Queen (1935)

#Africa #Hollywood #river #movies #UnitedStates

---

[8] Botanical point for horticultural name.
[9] Botanical point for horticulture name.

Aromatic plants bestow

No spicy fragrance while they grow;

But crush'd or trodden to the ground,

Diffuse their balmy sweets around.

Oliver Goldsmith (1728 – 1774)
Irish novelist, playwright, poet
"The Captivity, an oratorio, Act I" (1764)
#Ireland #songs #spices #theatre

On such heavenly nights I would sit for hours at my window inhaling the sweetness of the garden, and musing on the checkered fortunes of those whose history was dimly shadowed out in the elegant memorials around.

Washington Irving (1783 – 1859)
American author
The Alhambra: a series of tales and sketches of the Moors and Spaniards (1832)
#history #memorial #night #Spain #travel #UnitedStates

Hoyt's

German Cologne Advertising Poster (1850 – 1920).

… looking down the meadows, I could see a boy gathering Lilies and Lady—smocks, and there cropping Culverkeyes[10] and Cowslips, all to make Garlands suitable to this present month of May, these, and many other field—flowers, so perfumed the air, that I thought that very meadow, like the field in Sicily, of which Diodorus speaks, where the perfumes rising from the place, make all dogs that hunt in it to fall off, and to lose their hottest scent.

Izaak Walton (1594 – 1683)
English author
The Compleat Angler (1653)
#England #literature #perfume #Sicily #wildflowers

Nothing can beat the smell of dew and flowers and the odor that comes out of the earth when the sun goes down.

Ethel Waters (1896 – 1977)
American singer, actress
His Eye is on the Sparrow (1951)
#biography #dew #songs #soil #sunset #UnitedStates

---

[10] Any of various plants bearing bluebell-shaped flowers: such as a European herb (*Hyacinthoides nonscripta, Scilla nonscripta*) (Merriam-Webster 2011).

THERE IS SOMETHING IN YOU
LIKE SOMETHING IN ME

There is something in you like something in me:

Our hearts both leap when a man is brave,

And we bare our heads at the silent grave;

We both turn aside at an infant's cry;

We pause as the windlet's whispering sigh

Awakens the human chords within,

Like the minor tones of a violin.

It will always be;

For there is something in you like something in me.

There is something in me like something in you:

It is found in the calm beneath ripples and foam,

Midst the surgings of life, or in silence alone.

I pass, and I pluck from a violet bed,

And am cheered all day by the fragrance shed;

You pass, on your way, this bit of sky;

And pluck you a violet, the same as I.

This violet blue

Speaks to something in me like something in you.

There is something in me like something in you:

'Tis the spirit that blooms at the ebb of the year;

'Tis the love that is kindled by tokens of cheer,

You send me a gift you have worked with awhile—

A poem, a picture, a flower, a smile;

I send you a message, of which I'm a part;

I send you a song that is breathed from my heart,—

A gift, it is true,

Of something in me like something in you.

There is something in you like something in me:

We give it no name—perchance we may call

It the fragrance of life, that beautifies all,

Or the whisperings of love, or the great Master Soul

That will surge thru the worlds as the eons may roll,

When all else is gone, this something will live,

We will sing, then, and love, and abundantly give

Of this that is free—

This something in you like something in me.

L. W. Bartlett (unknown)
The National Magazine
Volume XLVI: (April 1917 to September 1917)
#friendship #kinship #poetry #UnitedStates

The studio was filled with the rich odour of roses, and when the light summer wind stirred amidst the trees of the garden, there came through the open door the heavy scent of the lilac, or the more delicate perfume of the pink–flowering thorn.

Oscar Wilde (1854 – 1900)
Irish author, playwright, poet
The Picture of Dorian Gray (1890)
#Ireland #literature #painting #perfume #trees #wind

I hope that while so many people are out smelling the flowers, someone is taking the time to plant some.

Herbert Rappaport (b. 1940)
Clinical psychologist
Holiday Blues: Rediscovering The Art Of Celebration (2000)
#exercise #mentalhealth #psychology #UnitedStates

Delicacy is to the mind what fragrance is to the fruit.

La delicatasse est a l'esprit ce que la saveur est au fruit

Achille Poincelot (b. 1822 – 18..)
French philosopher, author
Panthéon des femmes (1855)
#delicacy #France #fruit #mind

Yet, the smell of a Yahoo[11] continuing very offensive, I always keep my nose well stopped with rue, lavender, or tobacco leaves.

Jonathan Swift (1667 – 1745)

Irish author

Gulliver's Travels (1726)

#England #Ireland #offensive

The personality is to the man what the perfume is with the flowers.

Charles Michael Schwab (1862 – 1939)

American steel magnate, author

Succeeding with What You Have (1917)

#perfume #personality #UnitedStates

I don't want to turn any of this into poetry

but

you're so beautiful

flowers turn their heads to smell you.

Shane Koyczan (b. 1976)

Canadian poet

Visiting Hours (2005)

#beauty #Canada #literature #love #poetry

---

[11] A Yahoo is a legendary being that is filthy and with unpleasant habits. (Wikipedia, 2015)

The fragrance of white tea is the feeling of existing in the mists that float over waters; the scent of peony is the scent of the absence of negativity: a lack of confusion, doubt, and darkness; to smell a rose is to teach your soul to skip; a nut and a wood together is a walk over fallen Autumn leaves; the touch of jasmine is a night's dream under the nomad's moon.

C. JoyBell C. (ca. 1970)
American author, poet
Vade Mecum (2013)
#Autumn #metaphor #soul #tea #UnitedStates

I sent thee late a rosy wreath, Not so much hon'ring thee

As giving it a hope that there It could not withered be;

But thou thereon did'st only breathe, And sent'st it back to me,

Since when it grows and smells, I swear Not of itself, but thee.

Ben Jonson (1572 – 1637)
English playwright, poet
"To Celia" (1605)
"Volpone" (1605)
#comedy #England #infatuation #love #play #poetry #songs

(A MODEST REQUEST)

You ask me what flower I prefer,

And it takes but a moment to think,

For its perfume is like nothing else,

And the name of that same is a pink,

A red pink.

When you bid me to dine or to sup,

Or invite me to breakfast or lunch,

Put a knot of them under my nose,

And hand me, when leaving, the bunch,

The whole bunch!

James Thomas Fields[12] (1817 – 1881)
American publisher, editor, poet
"Pinks"
Ballads and Other Verses (1880)
#ballad #perfume #poetry #UnitedStates

---

[12] Botanical point for horticultural name.

Heliotrope. To be sowed in the spring. A delicious flower, but I suspect it must be planted in boxes and kept in the house in the winter. The smell rewards the care.

Thomas Jefferson (1743–1826)
Founding Father of the United States
Principal author of the Declaration of Independence
3rd President of the United States (1801 – 1809)
Thomas Jefferson's *Garden Book,* Appendix III (1766 – 1824)
#containers #greenhouse #Monticello #Spring #UnitedStates

I shall go in a week to Monticello....my situation there and taste, will lead me to ask for curious and hardy trees, than flowers. Of the latter a few of those remarkeable [sic] either for beauty or fragrance will be the limits of my wishes…

Thomas Jefferson (1743–1826)
Founding Father of the United States
Principal author of the Declaration of Independence
3rd President of the United States (1801 – 1809)
Extract from letter to Bernard McMahon (July 15, 1806)
#beauty #design #trees #Monticello #UnitedStates

I have recieved [sic] safely the extraordinary rattle of the rattle snake, as also the ~~leav~~ foliage of the Alleghaney Martagon. a plant of so much beauty & fragrance will be a valuable addition to our flower gardens.

Thomas Jefferson (1743–1826)
Founding Father of the United States
Principal author of the Declaration of Independence
3rd President of the United States (1801 – 1809)
Extract from letter to W. Fleming (November 28, 1809)
#beauty #design #Monticello #UnitedStates

I remember ~~you~~ [sic] seeing in your greenhouse a plant of a couple of feet height in a pot the fragrance of which (from it's [sic] gummy bud if I recollect rightly) was ~~remarkable~~ [sic] peculiarly agreeable to me, and you were so kind as to remark that it required only a green house, and that you would furnish me one when I should be in a situation to preserve it. but it's [sic] name has entirely escaped me.

Thomas Jefferson (1743–1826)
Founding Father of the United States
Principal author of the Declaration of Independence
3rd President of the United States (1801 – 1809)
Extract from letter to W. Hamilton (July 1806)
#beauty #greenhouse #Monticello #UnitedStates

There fragrant woodbines form'd a mantling bower;

And there I planted the luxuriant vine;

There love and friendship bless'd the festive hour,

While every rural happiness was mine.

Felicia Dorothea Browne Hemans (1793 – 1835)
English poet
"The Exile"[13]
Poems (1808)

#England #friendship #happiness #love

…whatsoever whether great or small ugly or handsom sweet or stinking as is commonly reputed but every thing in the universe in their own nature appears beautiful to me …

John Bartram Sr. (1699 – 1777)
American botanist, horticulturist, explorer
Letter to J. Slingsby Cressy, British physician in Antiqua[14]
"Bartram Papers 1:23:4" (March or April 1740)
#nature #UnitedStates #universe #WestIndies #wishlist

---

[13] Written when Felicia was between 8 and 13 years old. (Britannica, 2018)
[14] Bartram's response when asked by Dr. Cressy what kind of plants he would like to have from Antiqua. (Fry)

You all have a manure pile of memories. Nothing you can do about that. Now you can drown in the stink or turn it into compost and grow a garden.

Rebecca O'Donnell (b. 1961)
American author, confectionary artist
Freak: The True Story of an Insecurity Addict (2011)
#compost #memories #negativity #regret #UnitedStates

Sing on; before me gardens rise,

Rich with their scented bowers;

Once more each vanished footsteps flies

O'er verdant paths of flowers.

Catherine Ann Warfield (1816 – 1877)
Eleanor Percy Ware Lee (1819 – 1849)
Ameircan poets, writers, sisters
Wife of Leon and other poems (1844)
#poetry #walking #UnitedStates

The delicious month of May had now come round once more. Nature, awakening to life, put on its wondrous robe of many colors, and the sun in proud consciousness of its power to tempt with the alluring warmth, the flowers concealed in the mystic bosom of Mother Earth, shone with ever increasing fervency. In Central Park Nature's feathered choir poured forth its gay song into the lovely spring air, while the perfumed lilacs lavished their scent upon all who came, caring not whether the dweller in tenements breathed it in greedily, or whether the superior residents of Fifth Avenue ignored it contemptuously. In the house of the rich manufacturer the perfume of the lilacs was not missed; the most *recherché*[15] hot–house plants supplanting them in fragrance were artistically grouped on both sides of the great staircase down to the front door, filling all the room with a perfume that bewildered the senses. Servants in livery hastened busily, but noiselessly, about, putting the last touches to the decorations of the parlor for the wedding ceremony to be performed on this day. In the adjoining room a

---

[15] Rare, exotic, or obscure. (Watkins)

beautiful altar was visible, decked with superb flowers from which

festoons of myrtle ran up to a hanging bell of red and white roses.

Anne Goldmark Gross (b.1847 - unknown)
American author
The Gnomes of Saline Mountain (1912)
#fairies #gnomes #nature #NewYork #perfume #Spring

A skillful horticulturist will exhibit the most delicate shades of

fragrance in different species of rose, but the novice cannot but

realize to what a miraculous extent the most refined in nature may

be sublimated and modified; the same thing is practicable as

regards both hue and form.

Henry Theodore Tuckerman (1813 - 1871)
American critic, essayist, poet
The Optimist (1850)
#horticulture #nature #UnitedStates

For many people the scent of certain plants can revive memories with a vividness that nothing else can equal, for the sense of smell can be extraordinarily evocative, bringing back pictures as sharp as photographs of scenes that had left the conscious mind.

Thalassa Cruso (1909-1997)
English plant expert, author, PBS television host
The Gardening Year (1973)
#England #memories #photography #UnitedStates

…"Oh, mother—!" exclaimed the girl. "What?" said the woman, suspended in the act of putting the lamp glass over the flame. The copper reflector shone handsomely on her, as she stood with uplifted arm, turning to face her daughter. "You've got a flower in your apron!" said the child, in a little rapture at this unusual event. "Goodness me!" exclaimed the woman, relieved. "One would think the house was afire." She replaced the glass and waited a moment before turning up the wick. A pale shadow was seen floating vaguely on the floor. "Let me smell!" said the child, still rapturously, coming forward and putting her face to her mother's waist. "Go along, silly!" said the mother, turning up the lamp. The light revealed their suspense so that the woman felt it almost unbearable. Annie was still bending at her waist. Irritably, the mother took the flowers out from her apron-band. "Oh, mother—don't take them out!" Annie cried, catching her hand and trying to replace the sprig. "Such nonsense!" said the mother, turning away. The child put the pale chrysanthemums to her lips, murmuring: "Don't they smell beautiful!" Her mother gave a short laugh. "No," she said, "not to me. It was chrysanthemums when I married him, and chrysanthemums when you were born, and the first time they ever brought him home drunk, he'd got brown chrysanthemums in his button-hole."

David Herbert Lawrence (1885 – 1930)
English novelist, poet, playwright, essayist, literary critic, painter
"The Odour of Chrysanthemums"
The English Review (July 1911)
#England #family #innocence #life

As there are some flowers which you should smell but slightly to extract all that is pleasant in them, and which, if you do otherwise, emit what is unpleasant and noxious, so there are some men with whom a slight acquaintance is quite sufficient to draw out all that is agreeable; a more intimate one would be unsatisfactory and unsafe.

Walter Savage Landor (1775 – 1864)
English writer, poet, activist
Pericles and Aspasia (1836)
#acquaintances #enemies #England #humanity

What's in a name? That which we call a rose, by any other name would smell as sweet.

William Shakespeare (1515 – 1564)
English playwright, poet, actor
"Romeo and Juliet" (1597)
#England #play #Shakespeare #theatre

For these many years, since I have lived here in the country, I have had it in my mind to write something about the odour and taste of this well-flavoured earth. The fact is, both the sense of smell and the sense of taste; have been shabbily treated in the amiable rivalry of the senses. Sight and hearing have been the swift and nimble brothers, and sight especially, the tricky Jacob of the family, is keen upon the business of seizing the entire inheritance, while smell, like hairy Esau, comes late to the blessing, hungry from the hills, and willing to trade its inheritance for a mess of pottage.

David Grayson (pseudonym)
Ray Stannard Baker (1870-1946)
American journalist
Great Possessions: A New Series of Adventures (1917)
#blessings #bucolic #country #metaphor #OldTestament #UnitedStates

The sky was aquamarine, stroked with clouds. She could smell the grass and taste the scent of small, crushed flowers. She looked back up over her forehead at the gray-black wall towering behind her, and wondered if the castle had ever been attacked on days like this. Did the sky seem so limitless, the waters of the straits so fresh and clean, the flowers so bright and fragrant, when men fought and screamed, hacked and staggered and fell and watched their blood mat the grass?

Mists and dusk, rain and lowering cloud seemed the better background; clothes to cover the shame of battle.

Iain Banks (1954 – 2013)
Scottish author
Use of Weapons (1990)
#battle #Scotland #war #weapons

GARDENING WITH SIGHT

When you take a flower in your hand and really look at it, it's your world for the moment. I want to give that world to someone else. Most people in the city rush around so, they have no time to look at a flower. I want them to see it whether they want to or not.

Georgia O'Keeffe (1887 – 1986)
American artist
<u>New York Post</u> (May 16, 1946)
#painting #flowers #UnitedStates #urban

We must never lose hold of the principle that every flower is meant to be seen by human creatures with human eyes, as by spiders with spider eyes.

John Ruskin (1819 – 1900)
English art critic
Proserpina: Studies of Wayside Flowers (1875)
#art #England #perspective #principle #spiders #viewpoint

A garden is a delight to the eye and a solace for the soul.

Abū–Muhammad Muslih al–Dīn
bin Abdallāh Shīrāzī (1210 – ca.1291)[16]
Persian author, poet
The Gulistan (1258)
#beauty #Iran #Persia #poetry #soul

The Lely is an herbe wyth a whyte floure.

And though the levys of the floure be whyte:

yet wythin shyneth the lykenesse of golde.

Bartholomaeus Anglicus (ca. 1203 – 1272)
English Franciscan author, scholastic
De Proprietatibus Rerum (1240)
#Catholicism #education #England #gold #herbs #white

---

[16] Better known as Saadi (سعدی Sa'dī (Sa'di)

The real voyage of discovery consists, not in seeking new landscapes, but in having new eyes.

Marcel Proust (1871 – 1922)

French novelist, critic, essayist

Sodom et Gomorrhe III. La Prisonnière (1923)

#art #design #France #literature #passion #repetition #travel

Nobody sees a flower – really – it is so small it takes time – we haven't time – and to see takes time, like to have a friend takes time.

Georgia O'Keeffe (1887 – 1986)

American artist

New York Post (May 16, 1946)

#art #friendship #nature #painting #patience #size #UnitedStates

Look how the blue—eyed violets glance love to one another.

Thomas Buchanan Read (1822 – 1872)

American poet, portrait–painter

"Why Not We"

Poems (1847)

#love #passion #poetry #UnitedStates

Yet these sweet sounds of the early season,

And these fair sights of its sunny days,

Are only sweet when we fondly listen,

And only fair when we fondly gaze.

There is no glory in star or blossom,

Till looked upon by a loving eye;

There is no fragrance in April breezes,

Till breathed with joy as they wander by.

William Cullen Bryant (1794 – 1878)
American editor, journalist, poet
"An Invitation to the Country"
<u>Harper's Weekly</u> (May 1857)
#April #fragrance #joy #seasons #Spring #UnitedStates

There is that in the glance of a flower which may at times control

the greatest of creation's braggart lords.

John Muir (1838 – 1914)
Scottish–American naturalist, author, environmental philosopher
A Thousand–Mile Walk to the Gulf (1916)
#naturalism #philosophy #power #Scotland #UnitedStates

For I always think the flowers can see us, and know what we are

thinking about.

George Eliot (1819 – 1880)

English novelist, poet, journalist

Silas Marner (1861)

#England #insight #thought

How exquisitely sweet

This rich display of flowers

This airy wild of fragrance

So lovely to the eye,

And to sense sweet.

William Cowper (1731 – 1800)

English poet, hymnodist

"Adam: A Sacred Drama. Act 2" (1823)

#England #fragrance #play #poetry

Our last impression of her as she turned the corner was that smile,

flung backward like a handful of flowers.

Wallace Stegner (1909 – 1993)

American novelist, environmentalist, historian

Crossing to Safety (1987)

#friendship #life #literature #marriage #UnitedStates

Here's ivy! take them, as I used to do Thy flowers, and keep them where they shall not pine. Instruct thine eyes to keep their colours true, and tell thy soul, their roots are left in mine.

Elizabeth Barrett Browning (1806 – 1861)
English poet
Sonnets from the Portuguese (1850)
#colors #England #love #poetry

I came hoping to see those eyes, but instead I return with my heart, leaving behind only flowers.

Kim Dong Hwa (b. 1950)
Korean graphic book artist
The Color of Earth (2003)
#adulthood #art #comics #Korea #love #teenagers #women

One of the most attractive things about flowers is their beautiful reserve.

Henry David Thoreau (1817 – 1862)
American philosopher, author, naturalist
Journals, entry for June 17, 1853 (1906)
#beauty #control #UnitedStates

Seeing is not just about the gift of sight. It is about the dawning of a greater comprehension and deeper insight into a subject. Gardening is a profound holistic experience.

Jinny Blom[17] **(b. 1962)**
English garden designer, author
The Thoughtful Gardener (2017)
#England #holistic #insight #understanding

A wisely and purely educated virgin is so poetic a flower of this dull world, that the sight of this glorious blossom hanging some years after the honeymoon, with yellow, faded leaves, in unwatered beds, must grieve any man who beholds it with a poet's eye.

Jean Paul Friedrich Richter (1763 – 1825)
German Romantic writer, philosopher
Levana, or The Doctrine of Education (1807)[18]
#aging #education #Germany #life #philosophy #poetry #virginity

---

[17] Botanical point for horticultural name. Swedish, Danish, Norwegian and Afrikaans term for bloom or flower.
[18] *Levana order Erziehungslehre* (1807)

The garden — where such neatness met the eye,

A stranger could not pass unheeding by ;

The orchard — and the yellow–mantled fields,

Each in its turn some dear remembrance yields.

Rufus Dawes (1803 – 1859)
American law student, poet, government clerk
The Valley of The Nashaway and other poems (1830)
#design #memories #neatness #UnitedStates

Let us learn another lesson from the lily of the field. How small a portion of its exquisite beauty is within the reach of our vision. Look with a true heart and a loving spirit, study its wondrous mechanism, its faultless form, seek for the secret of its 'tender grace,' and when you have read all that eye can see, and have felt all that heart can receive, remember that you know but in part, that you see the beauty of this flower only through a glass darkly. It has a wealth of beauty that to you is entirely imperceptible.

Joseph Breck (1794 – 1873)
American Seedsman, Florist, Editor of the New England *Farmer*
The Flower-Garden, or *Breck's Book of Flowers* (1851)
#Eden #horticulture #nature #travel #UnitedStates

In short, Beauty is everywhere. It is not that she is lacking to our eye, but our eyes which fail to perceive her. Beauty is character and expression. Well, there is nothing in nature which has more character than the human body. In its strength and its grace it evokes the most varied images. One moment it resembles a flower: the bending torso is the stalk; the breasts, the head, and the splendor of the hair answer to the blossoming of the corolla. The next moment it recalls the pliant creeper, or the proud and upright sapling.

We need not compass sea and land for our gratification; the means for innocent healthy and relaxation within the reach of everyone. It lies around us; it is at our feet; "it may be found in the garden, where, in the beginning, everything pleasant to the sight", was congregated.

Joseph Breck (1794 – 1873)
American Seedsman, Florist, Editor of the New England Farmer
The Flower-Garden, or Breck's Book of Flowers (1851)
#Eden #horticulture #nature #travel #UnitedStates

CORN-FLOWER.

There is a flower whose
modest eye
Is turned with looks of
light and love,
Who breathes her softest,
sweetest sigh,
Whene'er the sun is
bright above.

"Artistic Language of Flowers." 1888. G. Routledge & sons

May we attribute to the color of the herbage and plants, which no doubt clothe the plains of Mars, the characteristic hue of that planet, which is noticeable by the naked eye, and which led the ancients to personify it as a warrior?

Camille Flammarion (1842 – 1925)
French astronomer and author
"Mars, by the Latest Observations"
<u>Popular Science</u> (Dec 1873)[19]
#France #color #doubt #Mars #planets #science

One of the pleasures of being a gardener comes from the enjoyment you get looking at other people's yards.

Thalassa Cruso (1909 – 1997)
English garden writer, celebrity horticulturist
To Everything There Is a Season: The Gardening Year (1973)
#England #neighbors #pleasure #seasons #walking

---

[19] First published in French as "La Planète Mars d'après les dernières observations astronomiques" in two parts in La Nature no. 10, 9 August 1873 and no. 11, 16 August 1873.

During the first nineteen months of my life I had caught glimpses of broad, green fields, a luminous sky, trees and flowers which the darkness that followed could not wholly blot out. If we have once seen, "the day is ours, and what the day has shown."

Helen Keller (1880 – 1868)
American author, political activist, lecturer
The Story of My Life: With Her Letters and a Supplementary Account of her Education (1903)
#biography #childhood #memories #nature #UnitedStates

The gold–eyed kingcups fine;

The frail bluebell peereth over

Rare broidry of the purple clover.

Let them rave.

Kings have no such couch as thine,

As the green that folds thy grave.

Let them rave.

Lord Alfred Tennyson (1809 – 1892)
British Poet Laureate
"A Dirge"
Poems Chiefly Lyrical (1830)
#England #death #funeral #poetry #wildflowers

The rose is a distilling eye. It gathers light and filters it until the concentration is powerful and pure, until its stamens become erect.

William H. Gass (1924 – 2017)
American novelist, short–story writer, essayist,
critic, philosophy professor
*READING RILKE: Reflections on the Problems of Translation (*1999)[20]
#literature #metaphor #novel #philosophy #passion #UnitedStates

O, the eye's light is a noble gift of heaven! All beings live from light; each fair created thing, the very plants, turn with a joyful transport to the light.

Johann Christoph Friedrich von Schiller (1759 – 1805)
German poet, philosopher, physician,
historian, playwright
"Wilhelm Tell" (1804)
#Germany #heaven #joy #theatre

---

[20] René Karl Wilhelm Johann Josef Maria Rilke, better known as Rainer Maria Rilke, was a Bohemian–Austrian poet and novelist. (1875– 1924) (Wikipedia)

I know, for thou hast told me,

Thy maiden love of flowers;

Ah, those that deck thy gardens

Are pale compared with ours.

When our wide woods and mighty lawns

Bloom to the April skies,

The earth has no more gorgeous sight

To show to human eyes.

In meadows red with blossoms,

All summer long, the bee

Murmurs, and loads his yellow thighs,

For thee, my love, and me.

William Cullen Bryant (1794 – 1898)

American poet, journalist,

New York Evening Post editor

"The Hunter's Serenade"

POEMS: by William Cullen Bryant, An American (1821)

#hunting #poetry #forest #UnitedStates

Flowers her eyes were, take me, willing eyes.

James Joyce (1881 – 1942)
Irish novelist, short story writer, poet, teacher, literary critic
Ulysses (1918 – 1920)
#Bloomsday[21] #Ireland #literature #love #passion

In the marshes the buckbean has lifted its feathery mist of flower spikes above the bed of trefoil leaves. The fimbriated flowers are a miracle of workmanship and every blossom exhibits an exquisite disorder of ragged petals finer than lace. But one needs a lens to judge of their beauty: it lies hidden from the power of our eyes, and menyanthes[22] must have bloomed and passed a million times before there came any to perceive and salute her loveliness. The universe is full of magical things patiently waiting for our wits to grow sharper.

Eden Phillpotts (1862 – 1960)
English author, poet and dramatist
A Shadow Passes (1919)
#beauty #England #magic #universe

---

[21] Bloomsday is a celebration that takes place both in Dublin and around the world. It celebrates Thursday 16 June 1904, which is the day depicted in James Joyce's novel Ulysses. The day is named after Leopold Bloom, the central character in Ulysses.

[22] The buckbean, bogbean; a genus of the *Gentinaceae*, so called because of its reputed menses properties. Native to North America. (Wikipedia, 2010)

To study culture, and with artful toil

To meliorate and tame the stubborn soil;

To give dissimilar yet fruitful lands

The grain or herb or plant that each demands;

To cherish virtue in an humble state,

And share the joys your bounty may create;

To mark the matchless workings of the power

That shuts within its seed the future flower,

Bids these in elegance of form excel,

In colour these, and those delight the smell,

Sends Nature forth, the daughter of the skies,

To dance on earth, and charm all human eyes.

William Cowper (1731 – 1800)
English poet, hymnodist
'Retirement'
Poems: by William Cowper, of the Inner Temple, Esq. (1782)
#culture #England #poetry #literature #retirement

In transient homes there are sure to be eyesores, ugly, ill–kept spots which we will want to hide from our own eyes and the knowledge of others. Morning glories and nasturtiums will rapidly respond to our call for help and under draperies of loveliness disguise the secrets of sordidness.

Hanna Rion Ver Beck (1875 – 1924)
American author, illustrator
Let's Make a Garden (1912)
#design #eyesore #neighbors #UnitedStates

To the eyes that have regained their sight, more wonder lies in the craftsmanship of a tiny leaf–form of inconsequential weed, than is to be found in a bombastic arras.

Hanna Rion Ver Beck (1875 – 1924)
American author, illustrator
Let's Make a Garden (1912)
#design #eyesore #neighbors #UnitedStates #weeds

Geoffrey Thorpe: You seem to be very fond of English roses.

Doña Maria: My mother told me about your rose gardens. She was English.

Geoffrey Thorpe: That explains a great deal.

Doña Maria: But I prefer the Spanish iris.

Geoffrey Thorpe: Naturally. It has no thorns.

Doña Maria: Capt. Thorpe, I didn't get a chance on the boat... but I want to thank you for returning my jewels. I'm so sorry for what I said about your robbing women. If you think it would do any good, I'd be glad to speak to the Queen. To tell her how kindly you treated us and that we don't want you punished.

Geoffrey Thorpe: That's very kind of you indeed. I think I can stand the punishment, but I'm very grateful for your concern. I wonder if you can imagine how much it means to me.

Doña Maria: No, I haven't any notion.

Geoffrey Thorpe: When I saw you first... I thought you were like a statue. Beautiful but cold. Then I watched you when you saw the slaves... and the statue seemed to come to life. I thought perhaps you'd forgive me one day.

Doña Maria: Capt. Thorpe, I have forgiven you.

Geoffrey Thorpe: Is forgiveness all you feel?

Doña Maria: Have I led you to believe anything else?

Geoffrey Thorpe: Not by anything you've said... but I thought I saw something in your eyes.

Doña Maria: No, you're mistaken.

Geoffrey Thorpe: I'm sorry.

Doña Maria: You're mistaken.

Geoffrey Thorpe: Perhaps that's as well, since I'm going back to sea.

Doña Maria: What?

Geoffrey Thorpe: We'll be gone quite some time.

Doña Maria: Are you leaving soon?

Geoffrey Thorpe: Within a week or so, just as soon as the Albatross is ready. The roses look different when you hold them. In the garden of a convent in Peru, there's a beautiful statue. The nuns call it Nuestra Senora de Las Flores.[23] That's how I'll always think of you, as my lady of the roses.

Geoffrey Thorpe (Errol Flynn)
Doña Maria (Brenda Marshall)
The Sea Hawk (1940)
Michael Curtiz, Director
Warner Brothers
Rafael Sabatini (1875 – 1950)
The Sea Hawk (1915)
Italian author
Turner Classic Movies (August 17, 2019)
#England #forgiveness #Hollywood #Italy #movies #pirates #Spain

HEAP not on this mound
Roses that she loved so well;
Why bewilder her with roses,
That she cannot see or smell ?
She is happy where she lies
With the dust upon her eyes.

Edna St. Vincent Millay (1892 – 1950)
American poet, playwright
'Epitaph'
Second April (1921)

#irony #poetry #UnitedStates

---

[23] Our Lady of the Flowers.

Though the New Year was approaching, the island was abloom with winter roses, and Rilke's[24] cottage, on the grounds of the villa, was covered with them.

Living in silence, endlessly unfolding,

using space without space being taken

from a space even trinkets diminish;

scarcely the hint there of outline or ground

they are so utterly in, so strangely delicate

and self–lit—to the very edge:

it possible we know anything like this?

And then like this: that a feeling arises

because now and then the petals kiss?

And this: that one should open like an eye,

to show more lids beneath, each closed

in a sleep as deep as ten, to quench

---

[24] René Karl Wilhelm Johann Josef Maria Rilke, better known as Rainer Maria Rilke, was a Bohemian–Austrian poet and novelist. (1875– 1924) (Wikipedia)

an inner fire of visionary power.

And this above all: that through these petals

light must make its way. Out of one thousand skies

they slowly drain each drop of darkness

so that this concentrated glow

will bestir the stamens till they stand.

William H. Gass (1924 – 2017)
American novelist, short–story writer, essayist,
critic, philosophy professor
*READING RILKE: Reflections on the Problems of Translation (*1999*)*
#literature #novel #philosophy #metaphor #passion #UnitedStates

There are philosophies as varied as the flowers of the field, and some of them weeds and a few of them poisonous weeds. But they, none of them create the psychological conditions in which I first saw, or desired to see, the flower.

G. K. Chesterton (1874 – 1936)
English journalist, novelist, essayist, poet, lay theologian
The Autobiography of G. K. Chesterton (1936)
#England #philosophy #weeds #wildflowers

When all my five and country senses see,

The fingers will forget green thumbs and mark

How, through the halfmoon's vegetable eye,

Husk of young stars and handfull zodiac,

Love in the frost is pared and wintered by.

Dylan Thomas (1914 – 1953)
Welsh poet, writer
"When All My Five And Country Senses See"
The Map of Love: Verse and Prose (1939)
#love #moon #vegetables #Wales #zodiac

GARDENING WITH SOUND

I was just sittin' here, enjoyin' the company. Plants have a lot to say, if you take the time to listen.

Eeyore (b. 1926)
Character in A. A. Milne's Winnie the Pooh
"The New Adventures of Winnie the Pooh"
"Rabbit Takes a Holiday/ Eeyi Eeyi Eeyore"
ABC Season 3 Episode 8 (Sep 29, 1990)
#Literature #children #television #UnitedStates

"Some people think plants can hear us,'' said the scientist.

"They can,'' said the celebrity[25].

Gza (b. 1966)
American Rapper, Wu–Tang Clan
"Science and The Genius"
Mary Carmichael, <u>The Boston Globe</u> (Dec 3, 2011)
#music #science #UnitedStates

What a pity flowers can utter no sound!

A singing rose, a whispering violet,

a murmuring honeysuckle—

oh, what a rare and exquisite miracle would these be!

Henry Ward Beecher (1811 – 1896)
American Congregationalist clergyman, social reformer, speaker
"Beecher: Christian Philosopher, Pulpit Orator, Patriot and Philanthropist:
A Volume of Representative Selections from the Sermons, Lectures,
Prayers, and Letters of Henry Ward Beecher" (1888)
#Christianity #miracles #sermon #music #UnitedStates

The hum of the bees is the voice of the garden.

Elizabeth Lawrence (1904 – 1985)
American horticultural writer, landscape architect
"Bees Dislike Strong Scent"
<u>Charlotte Observer</u> (August 30, 1959)
#bees #pollinators #humming #UnitedStates

---

[25] GZA – aka Gary Grice

I am well aware that she[26] enjoys listening to classical music, while decorating and gardening.

Edward Cullen (1901 - 1918)

Telepathic vampire

Stephanie Meyers (b. 1973)

American novelist

Twilight (2005)

#fiction #gothic #literature #UnitedStates #vampires

In nature we find silence — the trees, flowers, and grass grow in silence. The stars, the moon, and the sun move in silence.

Silence of the heart is necessary so you can hear God everywhere — in the closing of a door, in the person who needs you, in the birds that sing, in the flowers, in the animals.

Mother Teresa[27] (1910 – 1997)

Albanian Sister of Calcutta, Roman Catholic nun,

founder of Missionary Charities

In the Heart of the World: Thoughts, Stories, and Prayers (1997)

#Albania #astronomy #Catholicism #India #wildlife

---

[26] Bella Swan Cullen, Edward's wife.
[27] Honored as Saint Teresa of Calcutta.

Anything will give up its secrets if you love it enough. Not only have I found that when I talk to the little flower or to the little peanut they will give up their secrets, but I have found that when I silently commune with people they give up their secrets also – if you love them enough.

George Washington Carver (1861 – 1943)
American scientist
George Washington Carver in His Own Words (1991)
#love #science #secrets #UnitedStates

It seems to me as a woman's face doesn't want flowers; it's almost like a flower itself... It's like when a man's singing a good tune, you don't want t' hear bells tinkling and interfering wi' the sound.

George Eliot (1819 – 1880)
English writer, poet, journalist
Adam Bede (1860)
#England #literature #courtship #songs

Gimli halted and stooped to the ground. 'I hear nothing but the night-speech of plants and stone,' he said. 'Come! Let us hurry! The others are out of sight.'

J. R. R. Tolkien (1892 – 1973)
English writer, poet, philologist, teacher
The Fellowship Of The Ring (1954)
#England #fiction #literature #night

I could hear you, talking to the daffodils and tulips, whispering to the fairies that lived inside their petals. Each separate flower had a different family inside it.

Lucy Christopher (b. 1981)
British–Australian author
Stolen: A Letter to My Captor (2009)
#Australia #GreatBritain #fairies #family

As a gardener, I wonder if flowers really can't speak or just exercise unfailing good judgment in the matter.

Robert Brault (b. 1938)
American journalist, author
Round Up The Usual Suspects Thoughts on Just About Everything (2014)
#judgement #wonder #UnitedStates

DO PLANTS PRODUCE SOUNDS,
AND DO THEY "LISTEN?"

That plants produce sound waves has been known for some time. Specifically, plants emit sound waves at the lower end of the audio range within 10–240 Hz (audio acoustic emissions) as well as ultrasonic acoustic emissions (UAE) ranging from 20 to 300kHz. Over the last 45 years, these acoustic emissions (and particularly the UAE) have been measured and described several times (Milburn and Johnson 1966; Tyree and Sperry 1989; Kikuta et al. 1997; Laschimke et al. 2006). Acoustic emissions are generally interpreted as the result of the abrupt release of tension in the water–transport system of plants following cavitation as water is pulled by transpiration from the roots through the xylem to the leaves (Cohesion Theory, Dixon and Joly 1895; Zimmerman 1983). Cavitation occurs when dissolved air within the water expands in the xylem conduits, eventually generating air bubbles (embolism), occluding the conduits and making them unavailable to transport water (reviewed by Tyree and Sperry 1989). In this context, these acoustic signals are simply emitted as an incidental by–product of the physiological/biomechanical process of cavitation and in fact, many authors have conveniently used them as an indicator of cavitation, particularly in drought–stressed plants (Peña and Grace 1986; Raschi et al. 1989; Jackson and Grace 1996; Qiu et al. 2002; Perks et al. 2004; Rosner et al. 2006). Nonetheless, others have argued that these plant sounds are not caused by cavitation disruption of the stressed water column, but rather, that they are induced by a largely stable bubble system of the xylem conduits capable of transporting water in travelling peristaltic waves (Laschimke et al. 2006). Although it remains undisputed that cavitation can induce acoustic emissions, the acoustic signals emitted by plants are so numerous that it always seemed extremely unlikely that each acoustic event was attributable to cavitation alone (Raschi et al. 1990; Zimmermann et al. 2004; Laschimke et al. 2006) and in fact, recent evidence now indicates that plants generate sounds independently of dehydration and cavitation–related processes (Gagliano, Mancuso, et al. 2012). The mechanics of how plants produce sounds are still unknown. Plants are unlikely to possess the specialized morphological structures and/or organs that animals have evolved to produce sound; nonetheless, the biophysical principles at the cellular and molecular level may not be so dissimilar and in this context, the fundamental mechanism of sound production across all eukaryotes may be highly conserved. I propose here a putative model to start examining this phenomenon. Initially, we need to consider that sound waves are generated by objects that vibrate and in all eukaryotes, cells and their components vibrate as a result of intracellular motions generated by cellular processes such as the activity of motor proteins and the cytoskeleton (Howard 2009); cytoplasmic streaming represented by the orange arrows). Specifically, motor proteins such as myosins, a family of mechanochemical enzymes, use chemical energy derived from the hydrolysis of adenosine triphosphate in actin filaments to generate mechanical motion and hence vibrations. Using atomic force microscopes, such nanomechanical motions have been measured in different systems from vertebrate cardiomyocytes (i.e., heart cells, Domke et al. 1999) and auditory hair cells (i.e., spontaneous oscillations that play a role in active amplification of weak sounds in hearing, Jülicher 2001) to tiny microbial cells (e.g., the baker's yeast, *Saccharomyces cerevisiae*, with motions in the order of 0.8–1.6kHz; Pelling et al. 2004). Because cells are imbedded in a tissue and hence surrounded by other cells, individual cells are affected by the mechanical property of neighboring ones and this eventually builds up into a collective mode (i.e., coherent excitation, see Pokorný 1999); and results in the amplification of the signal. In plants, the radiated power of numerous cells working in such a concerted way has been theoretically predicted to be sufficient for observable effects, leading to acoustic flows in the order of 150–200kHz (Perelman and Rubinstein 2006). If such mechanical vibrations or sound waves can extend over large distances within the organism and also outside the organism, then the possibility arises that plants may actually use sound to communicate with other plants or organisms. Whichever explanation for the origin of acoustic emissions from plants is correct, the fact remains that plants emit sounds and they "hear" them too. Indeed, besides the folkloristic and at times esoteric reports of the influence of sound, and more specifically music, on plants (Backster 1968; Tompkins and Bird 1973), decades of scientific research indicate that plants do respond to sound waves of different frequencies by modifying germination and growth rates (Klein and Edsall 1965; Weinberger and Burton 1981; Takahashi et al. 1992).

Dr. Monica Gagliano (c. 1980's)
Australian Research Fellow, University of Sydney
"Green Symphonies: a call for studies on
acoustic communication in plants" (2013)
#acoustics #Australia #listen #research #science

Relax! Spring is just around the corner for Atlanta. Soon, you will be sprawled in a lawn chair, soaking in the sunshine, getting a marvelous tan...listening to the crabgrass grow.

Lou Bernard Erickson (1913 – 1990)
American editorial cartoonist
The Atlanta Constitution (March 5, 1978)
#newspaper #Spring #UnitedStates #weeds

I love to think of nature as unlimited broadcasting stations, through which God speaks to us every day, every hour and every moment of our lives, if we will only tune in and remain so.

George Washington Carver (1864 – 1943)
American scientist
Letter to Hubert W. Pelt (February 24, 1930)
"How to Search for Truth."
"George Washington Carver: In His Own Words." (1987)
#broadcasting #God #nature #UnitedStates

More and more as we come closer and closer in touch with nature and its teachings are we able to see the Divine and are therefore fitted to interpret correctly the various languages spoken by all forms of nature about us.

George Washington Carver (1864 – 1943)
American scientist
Letter to Hubert W. Pelt[28] (February 24, 1930)
"How to Search for Truth."
"George Washington Carver: In His Own Words." (1987)
#God #language #nature #science #spirituality #UnitedStates

---

[28] Pelt Stokes Fund

…research has shown that plants do have pretty good awareness of their surroundings. For example, they can "hear" when they're being chewed on by insects, and release chemicals to stop it. And they're also able to communicate with each other via a subterranean "internet" of fungus.

Olivier Van Aken (ca. 1980)
Lead researcher, Sr. Lecturer, Lund University
Fiona MacDonald, ScienceAlert (May 31, 2016)
#awareness #Australia #research #science #sensitivity

The flowers continue the dialogues with him through the graceful bending of their stems and the harmoniously tinged shades of their flowers. Each flower has a cordial word that nature directs to it.[29]

Auguste Rodin (1840 – 1917)
French sculptor
Art (1912)
#art #communication #France #friendship #nature #protection #trees

---

[29] Correct English translation of French passage.

Who that has loved knows not the tender tale

Which flowers reveal, when lips are coy to tell?

Sir Edward George Earle Lytton Bulwer–Lytton (1803 – 1873)

English writer, politician.

"The First Violets"

The Poetical and Dramatical Works of Sir Edward Bulwer–Lytton (1854)

#England #secrets #symbolism

Flowers have spoken to me more than I can tell in written words. They are the hieroglyphics of angels, loved by all men for the beauty of their character, though few can decipher even fragments of their meaning.

Lydia Maria Child (1802 – 1880)

American abolitionist, activist, novelist

Letters from New York (1843)

#beauty #character #hieroglyphics #literature #meaning #UnitedStates

As a gardener, I wonder if flowers really can't speak or just exercise unfailing good judgment in the matter.

Robert Brault (b. 1938)

American journalist, author

Round Up The Usual Suspects Thoughts on Just About Everything (2014)

#fairytales #imagination #life #UnitedStates

"Not Seeing Is A Flower" is a Japanese proverb used as inspiration for the site-specific window installation designed and created by Whitney Lynn Studios that employs *floriography*, a form of cryptographic communication historically used as a means to communicate messages otherwise difficult to speak aloud. The flowers in the composition all have a relationship to countries affected by the travel ban and the dense collage includes official national flowers, native plants, and images appropriated from Colonial-era postage stamps.

Whitney Lynn (b. 1980)
American contemporary artist
Window Mural Installation
San Diego International Airport, San Diego, California (2018)
#architecture #art #communication #politics #sight #UnitedStates #world

Talk, said Holmes, is 'to me only spading up the ground for crops of thought.

Sir Leslie Stephen (1832 – 1904)
English author, critic, historian, biographer, mountaineer[30],[31]
Studies of a Biographer (1898)
#crops #England #soil #preparation #tilling

It seems to me that if a little flower could speak, it would tell simply what God has done for it without trying to hide its blessings. It would not say, under the pretext of a false humility, it is not beautiful and without perfume, that the sun has taken away its splendor and the storm has broken its stem when it knows that all this is untrue. The flower about to tell her story rejoices at having to publish the totally gratuitous gifts of Jesus. She knows that nothing in herself was capable of attracting the divine glances, and His mercy alone brought about everything that is good in her.

St. Thérèse of Lisieux (1873 – 1897)
French Catholic Discalced Carmelite nun
Saint, Doctor of the Catholic Church
*Story of a Soul (*1898)
#biography #Catholicism #France #mercy #perfume #religion #saints

---

[30] Father of Virginia Woolff and Vanessa Bell, both members of the Bloomsbury[19] Group.
[31] Botanical point for group horticultural name.

THE SERPENT: The voice in the garden is your own voice.

ADAM: It is; and it is not. It is something greater than me: I am only a part of it.

EVE: The Voice does not tell me not to kill you. Yet I do not want you to die before me. No voice is needed to make me feel that.

ADAM: [throwing his arm round her shoulder with an expression of anguish]: Oh no: that is plain without any voice. There is something that holds us together, something that has no word —

THE SERPENT: Love. Love. Love.

ADAM: That is too short a word for so long a thing.

George Bernard Shaw (1856–1950)
Anglo–Irish playwright, critic
"In the Beginning "Adam and Eve – Back to Methuselah" (1922)
#England #eternity #love #play #theatre

TO PHŒBE

"Gentle, modest little flower,

Sweet epitome of May,

Love me but for half an hour,

Love me, love me, little fay."

Sentences so fiercely flaming

In your tiny, shell–like ear,

I should always be exclaiming

If I loved you, Phœbe dear.

William Schwenk Gilbert (1836 – 1911)
English dramatist, librettist, poet, illustrator
The Bab Ballads (1868)
#ballads #children #England #metaphor #Spring

Everything is blooming most recklessly; if it were voices instead of colors, there would be an unbelievable shrieking into the heart of the night.

Rainer Maria Rilke (1875 – 1926)
Bohemian–Austrian poet, novelist
Briefe an einen jungen Dichter (1929)[32]
#Austria #color #Hungary #nature #noise #Spring

With fragrant breath the lilies woo me now, and softly speaks the sweet—voiced mignonette.

Julia Caroline Ripley Dorr (1825 – 1913)
American poet
"Without and Within"
Sonoma Democrat, Volume XV, Number 23, (March 16, 1872)
#courtship #UnitedStates

Say it with flowers.

Major Patrick O'Keefe (1872–1934)
Boston advertising agency CEO
Henry Penn (1877 – 1968)
Society of American Florists
Slogan coined for the Society of American Florists (1917)
#advertising #florists #gifts #slogan #UnitedStates

---

[32] English translation: *Letters to A Young Poet*

An Assist from Shakespeare on "Say It with Flowers"

THEODORE E. ASH

ADVERTISING

PHILADELPHIA, Jan. 9, 1922.

Editor of PRINTERS' INK:

I was greatly interested in your article in the December 22 number of PRINTERS' INK in which you gave credit as the creator of "Say It with Flowers" to Henry Penn, the Boston florist. You say, however, that Mr. Penn passed the honor along to a member of a Boston advertising agency who coined the expression four years ago and presented it at a meeting of the publicity committee of the Society of American Florists at Cleveland in 1917.

You seemed to have started something, as Sherley Hunter, of the George L. Dyer Company, writes that he used the expression first when he wrote the advertising for Darling's Flower Shop of Los Angeles in 1911. This would make the expression at least eleven years old.

Now I want to put in my oar and stir up the animals. I used the expression fifteen years ago in advertising I prepared for Charles Henry Fox, the florist, of Philadelphia. Mr. Fox copyrighted the name "Flowergram," and I used the slogan "Send a Flowergram" and "Say It with a Flowergram" for some time. Mr. Fox then became the leading spirit in promoting a cooperative campaign of newspaper advertising on flowers, and I was asked to write, and did write, a series of ads which appeared in several Philadelphia newspapers several times a week for nearly two years. These ads were financed by The Philadelphia Retail Florists' Association and were the first ads of a co-operative nature about flowers used in this country. I syndicated them to a number of florist associations and also to a number of individual florists throughout the United States and Canada.

As Mr. Fox wanted to retain the rights of "Flowergram" for his personal use, we simplified the expression from "Say It with a Flowergram" to "Say It with Flowers" when we used it in the association's copy. This makes the origin, therefore, date back fifteen years.

Personally, I want to give credit to Shakespeare as the originator. I borrowed my pet expression from him, namely, "Flowers speak what words never can." I used that expression oftener than "Say It with Flowers," and I got my idea of the "Say It with Flowers" from Bill.

I always thought Charles Henry Fox and I, jointly, used "Say It with Flowers" first, but it's dollars to doughnuts someone will come along and spill the beans for us. Let's get it over with, however, and as soon as possible.

THEODORE E. ASH.

THE LANGUAGE OF FLOWERS

In Eastern lands they talk in flow'rs

And they tell in a garland their loves and cares;

Each blossom that blooms in their garden bowr's,

On its leaves a mystic language bears.

The rose is a sign of joy and love,

Young blushing love in its earliest dawn,

And the mildness that suits the gentle dove,

From the myrtle's snowy flow'rs is drawn.

Innocence gleams in the lily's bell,

Pure as the heart in its native heaven.

Fame's bright star and glory's swell

By the glossy leaf of the bay are given.

The silent, soft and humble heart,

In the violet's hidden sweetness breathes,

And the tender soul that cannot part,

In a twine of evergreen fondly wreathes.

The cypress that daily shades the grave,

Flowers are Love's truest language; they betray,

Like the divining–rods of Magi old,

Where precious wealth lies buried, not of gold,

But love,—strong love, that never can decay!

I send thee flowers, O dearest! and I deem

That from their petals thou wilt hear sweet words,

Whose music, clearer than the voice of birds,

When breathed to thee alone, perchance, may

seem

All eloquent of feelings unexpressed.

O, wreathe them in those tresses of dark hair!

Let them repose upon thy forehead fair,

And on thy bosom's yielding snow be pressed!

Thus shall thy fondness for my flowers reveal

The love that maiden coyness would conceal!

Park Benjamin, Sr. (1809 – 1864)
American poet, journalist, newspaper editor
The Book of the Sonnet (1867)
#courtship #coyness #florist #love #Magi #UnitedStates

Once I spoke the language of the flowers,

Once I understood each word the caterpillar said,

Once I smiled in secret at the gossip of the starlings,

And a conversation with the housefly

in my bed.

Once I heard and answered all the questions

of the crickets,

And joined the crying of each falling dying

flake of snow,

Once I spoke the language of the flowers. . . .

How did it go?

How did it go?"

Shel Silverstein (1930 – 1990)

American author, poet, cartoonist, songwriter, playwright

Where the Sidewalk Ends (1974)

#childhood #children #imagination #poetry #UnitedStates

Is sorrow that moans her bitter lot,

And faith that a thousand ills can brave,

Speaks in thy blue leaves "forget–me–not".

Then gather a wreath from the garden bowers,

And tell the wish of thy heart in flowers.

James Gates Percival (1795 – 1856)
American geologist, poet, surgeon
"The Language of Flowers" (written in 1872)[33]
#language #love #UnitedStates

That flowers have a language is a fact I've noted long ;

But I must say that I never knew their voices were so strong.

Peter Sheaf Hersey Newell[34] (1864 – 1924)
American artist, writer
"A Borrowed Voice"
Peter Newell's Pictures and Rhymes (1899)
#art #language #nurseryrhymes #UnitedStates

---

[33] Unpublished poem.
[34] Botanical point for horticultural name.

Through the grass the little mosspaths, bony with old roots, and the trees sticking up, and the flowers sticking up, and the fruit hanging down, and the white exhausted butterflies, and the birds never the same darting all day long into hiding. And all the sounds, meaning nothing.

Samuel Beckett (1906 – 1989)
Irish novelist, playwright, theatre director, poet
Watt (1953)
#birds #butterflies #forest #Ireland

The temple bell stops

but I still hear the sound

coming out of the flowers.

Matsuo Bashō[35] (1644 – 1694)
Japanese poet
trans. Robert Bly
The Sea and the Honeycomb: A Book of Tiny Poems (1971)
#haiku #Japan #loneliness #sabi[36] #silence

---

[35] Bashō means banana. Matsuo loved his banana tree so much, he took the plant's name for himself. (Stryk, 1984)
[36] Sabi means *"to lean or withered, a flower past its bloom."* (Stryk, 1984)

GARDENING WITH TASTE

It is a pleasure to eat of the fruit of one's toil, if it be nothing more than a head of lettuce or an ear of corn.

Charles Dudley Warner (1829 – 1900)
American essayist, novelist
My Summer In A Garden (1870)
#agriculture #diary #farmtotable #labor #Summer #UnitedStates

Training is everything. The peach was once a bitter almond; cauliflower is nothing but cabbage with a college education.

Mark Twain (1835 – 1910)
American writer, humorist, entrepreneur, publisher, lecturer
Pudd'nhead Wilson's Calendar
Pudd'nhead Wilson (1893–1894)
#college #culture #diary #education # #slavery #society #UnitedStates

"A milkweed, and a buttercup, and cowslip," said sweet Mary,
"Are growing in my garden–plot, and this I call my dairy."

Peter Sheaf Hersey Newell (1864 – 1924)
American artist, writer
"My Dairy"
Peter Newell's Pictures and Rhymes (1899)
#art #dairy #plots #nurseryrhymes #UnitedStates #wildflowers

I know I ought to keep away from that garden," said Peter very meekly, "but you have no idea what a temptation it is. The things in that garden do taste so good.

Peter Rabbit
Thornton Burgess (1874 – 1965)
American conservationist and author
The Burgess Animal Book for Children (1920)
#children #literature #UnitedStates #wildlife

Good husbandry with us consists in abandoning Indian corn, and tobacco, tending small grain, some red clover, fallowing, and endeavoring to have, while the lands are at rest, a spontaneous cover of white clover. I do not present this as a culture judicious in itself, but as good in comparison with what most people there pursue.

Thomas Jefferson (1743–1826)
Founding Father of the United States
Principal author of the Declaration of Independence
3rd President of the United States (1801 – 1809)
'Letter to George Washington,' (June 28, 1793)
#agriculture #covercrops #farm #Monticello #UnitedStates

I inclose [sic] you some seeds of the *Acacia Farnesiana* the most delicious flowering shrub in the world.

Thomas Jefferson (1743–1826)
Founding Father of the United States
Principal author of the Declaration of Independence
3rd President of the United States (1801 – 1809)
'Letter to Bernard McMahon, Betts,' (Mar 30, 1792)
#edible #Monticello #seeds #UnitedStates

Beneath some orange–trees,

Whose fruit and blossoms in the breeze

Were wantoning together free,

Like age at play with infancy.

Thomas Moore (1779 – 1852)
Irish poet, singer, songwriter, entertainer
"Paradise and the Peri"
Lalla Rookh[37] *an Oriental Romance* (1817)

#infancy #fruit #Ireland #poetry #prose

Piscator, 'Tis enough, honest scholar! come, let's to supper. Come, my friend Coridon, this Trout looks lovely; it was twenty–two inches when it was taken; and the belly of it looked, some part of it, as yellow as a marigold, and part of it as white as a lily; and yet, methinks, it looks better in this good sauce.

Izaak Walton (1594 – 1683)
English author
The Compleat Angler (1653)
#England #fishing #history #supper

---

[37] *Lala Rukh* means "tulip-cheeked" in Persian and is used as an affectionate term in poetry. (Balfur)

Minnow–Tansies Recipe

...for being washed well in salt, and their heads and tails cut off, and their guts taken out, and not washed after, they prove excellent for that use, that is, being fried with yolks of eggs, the flowers of cowslips, and of primroses, and a little Tansie, thus used they make a dainty dish of meat.

Izaak Walton (1594 – 1683)
English author
The Compleat Angler (1653)
#England #fishing #history #literature #Italy #wildflowers

"Doubtless God could have made a better berry, but doubtless God never did;" and so, if I might be judge, God never did make a more calm, quiet, innocent recreation than angling.

Izaak Walton (1594 – 1683)
English author
The Compleat Angler (1653)
#England #fishing #history #literature #Italy #wildflowers

We may say of angling as Dr. Boteler said of strawberries,

Like strawberry wives, that laid two or three great strawberries

at the mouth of their pot, and all the rest were little ones.

Sir Francis Bacon (1561–1626)
English philosopher, statesman, scientist, essayist, author
A collection of apophthegms, new and old (1625)
#containers #England #fruit #size

The strawberry grows underneath the nettle

And wholesome berries thrive and ripen best

Neighbour'd by fruit of baser quality.

William Shakespeare (1564 – 1616)
English actor, playwright, poet
"Henry V" (c. 1599)
#England #fruit #play #quality #Shakespeare #theatre

A Man called Strawberry

We owe our juicy strawberries to a French spy and firework expert named Amédée–François Frézier (1682–1773). Dispatched in 1712 to assess the quality of the Spanish army's defensive fortifications in Chile, he returned with a new variety of strawberry (now called *Fragaria chiloensis*) which had been cultivated for many years by the Chilean Indians. He brought five specimen plants back to France, caring for them throughout his six–month journey home by feeding them his own precious supply of fresh water. From them, all the large, sweet strawberry varieties we enjoy today ultimately derive.

Oddly enough, Frézier's surname is itself derived from fraise, the French word for strawberry. His ancestor, Julius de Berry[38] (honestly) was bestowed the nickname in 916 after he presented the emperor with a gift of ripe (though not very juicy) strawberries.

Molly Oldfield (b. 1979)
British author, columnist, researcher
John Mitchinson (b.1961)
British author, researcher
QI [39], <u>The Telegraph</u> (September 10, 2012)
#Chile #England #France #fruit #newspaper #research #Telegraph #trivia

---

[38] Botanical point for horticultural name.

[39] Author's note: 'Quite Interesting,' a British comedy panel game television quiz show.

Figs were regarded with such esteem that laws were created forbidding the export of the best quality figs. *Sycophant* then derives from the Greek word meaning one who informs against another for exporting figs or for stealing the fruit of the sacred fig trees. Hence, the word came to mean a person who tries to win favor with flattery.

California Figs (2013)

#California #export #etymology #flattery #fruit
#Greece #history #law #quality #UnitedStates

And They Shall Beat Their Swords Into Plowshares

What should the farmer know in order to be truly successful? First, he must know cattle, their habits, their food, and what cattle will bring him the most economic and best returns in milk and in beef ; the practical and best food to give them ; the economical handling of food. He must know horses from a horseman's standpoint, from a farmer's standpoint. Pigs must be common knowledge to him.

He should be familiar with the infinite housekeeping details of chicken–raising, and the same for ducks and turkeys. He must know how to raise oats, wheat, com, rye, buckwheat, potatoes, alfalfa, timothy[40], clover.

The infinite secrets of the soil can not all be secrets to him. He

---

[40] Timothy is the common name for *Phleum pretense*, a grass. Name is thought to be attributed to Timothy Hanson, an American farmer and agriculturalist who introduced it up and down the East coast from New England to the southern states in the early 18th century. [Wikipedia]

must know the chemistry of the soil, and when, where and how seeds must be planted to get their nourishment from the soil.

He must know edible roots for cattle.

He must know garden vegetables and gardening.

He must know architecture and construction enough to supervise the building of a house, barns, and sheds, that shall best serve his needs.

And he must know economics. No other per son on earth needs to have so broad and generous an understanding of the subject of economics as does the farmer.

Let the cost of living aviate, let it soar, until the best intelligence, the most ambitious, the most aspiring of the human race shall realize that it is worth while to till the soil, to become in love with Mother Nature.

Our hope today is with the farmer.

Alice Hubbard (1861 – 1915)
American feminist, writer
"The Fra: For Philistines and Roycrofters" (August 1913)
#agriculture #farm ##soil #success #UnitedStates

"I shall find the black tulip," said Cornelius to himself, whilst detaching the suckers. "I shall obtain the hundred thousand guilders offered by the Society. I shall distribute them among the poor of Dort; and thus the hatred which every rich man has to encounter in times of civil wars will be soothed down, and I shall be able, without fearing any harm either from Republicans or Orangists, to keep as heretofore my borders in splendid condition. I need no more be afraid lest on the day of a riot the shopkeepers of the town and the sailors of the port should come and tear out my bulbs, to boil them as onions[41] for their families, as they have sometimes quietly threatened when they happened to remember my having paid two or three hundred guilders for one bulb.

Alexandre Dumas (1802 – 1870)

French writer

La Tulipe Noire (1850)[42]

#bulb #civilwar #France #rare #riot #substitution

---

[41] Tulips can be substituted for onions in cooking but remove the yellow core before cooking. (Deane, 2011)

[42] English translation: The Black Tulip.

The 1967 Florida State Legislature declared "the juice obtained from mature oranges of the species *Citrus sinensis* and hybrids are hereby adopted as the official beverage of the State of Florida."

Florida Statute *15.032*.
Florida History Network (April 16, 1967)
#Florida #state #fruit #law

Yet, whenever food or fire or courage failed, the simplest remedy in the world for every trouble was to go in haste to Master Simon Radpath. His grassy meadow was always green, his fields rich every harvest time with bowing grain, his garden always crowded with herbs and vegetables, and gay the whole summer long with flowers, scarlet and white and yellow.

Cornelia Meigs (1884 – 1973)
American writer, teacher, historian, critic
Master Simon's Garden (1916)
#herbs #history #Plymouth #Puritans #Summer
#UnitedStates #vegetables

It is strange what a taste you suddenly have for things you never liked before. The squash has always been to me a dish of contempt; but I eat it now as if it were my best friend. I never cared for the beet or the bean; but I fancy now that I could eat them all, tops and all, so completely have they been transformed by the soil in which they grew.

Charles Dudley Warner (1829 – 1900)
American essayist, novelist
A Summer in A Garden (1870)
#meals #Summer #UnitedStates #vegetables

Sagebrush is a very fair fuel, but as a vegetable it is a distinguished failure. Nothing can abide the taste of it but the jackass and his illegitimate child the mule.

Mark Twain (1835 – 1910)
American writer, humorist, entrepreneur, publisher, lecturer
Roughing It (1891)
#desert #UnitedStates #vegetables #West

Cabbage: A familiar kitchen–garden vegetable about as large and wise as a man's head.

Ambrose Bierce (1842 – 1914)
American short story writer, journalist, poet
The Cynic's Word Book (1911)
#definition #kitchengardens #UnitedStates #vegetables

I remember a time when a cabbage could sell itself by being a cabbage. Nowadays it's no good being a cabbage – unless you have an agent and pay him a commission. Nothing is free anymore to sell itself or give itself away. These days, Countess, every cabbage has its pimp.

Jean Giraudoux (1882 – 1944)
French novelist, essayist, diplomat, playwright.
The Madwoman of Chaillot (1943)
#corruption #France #play #satire #theatre #vegetables

When asked if he[43] liked vegetables: "I don't know. I have never eaten them… No, that is not quite true. I once ate a pea."

Lewis Melville (1780 – 1840)
English author
Beau Brummell, His Life and Letters (1924)
#biography #England #vegetables

---

[43] Beau Brummel

Odd as I am sure it will appear to some, I can think of no better form of personal involvement in the cure of the environment than that of gardening. A person who is growing a garden, if he is growing it organically, is improving a piece of the world. He is producing something to eat, which makes him somewhat independent of the grocery business, but he is also enlarging, for himself, the meaning of food and the pleasure of eating.

Wendell Berry (b. 1934)
American novelist, poet, essayist, farmer
The Art of the Commonplace: The Agrarian Essays (2002)
#food #grocery #organic #pleasure #UnitedStates

Celery is as fresh and clean as a rainy day after a spell of heat. It crackles pleasantly in the mouth… it should be eaten alone, for it's the only food which one really wants to hear oneself eat.

A. A. Milne (1882 – 1956)
American author
"A Word for Autumn"
Not That It Matters (1920)
#Summer #UnitedStates #vegetables

"I, Raoul Tanquy, who never was drunk

(Or hardly more than judge or monk,)

On fourth of July finished this book,

Then to drink at the Tabouret myself took,

With Pylon and boon companions more

Who tripe with onions and garlic adore."

Unknown transcriber (ca. 15th century)

An Explicit[44] found in an early fifteenth century copy of a Froissart[45] work

Arts and Crafts in the Middle Ages (1908)

#books #transcription #MiddleAges

by my new banana plant

the first sign of something I loathe—

a miscanthus bud!

Matsuo Bashō (1644 – 1694)

Japanese poet

(written in 1680)

Basho: The Complete Haiku, trans Jane Reichhold (2008)

#fruit #haiku #Japan #poetry #UnitedStates #weeds

---

[44] Explicit: the closing words of a text, manuscript, early printed book, or chanted liturgical text. (Dictionary.com, 2015)

[45] Jean Froissant, (1337 – 1405) French medieval poet, court historian. Wrote *Chronicles of the 14th Century*, which remains the most important and detailed document of feudal times in Europe and the best contemporary exposition of chivalric and courtly ideals. (Britannica, 2019)

The herb feeds upon the juice of a good soil, and drinks in the dew of heaven as eagerly, and thrives by it as effectually, as the stalled ox that tastes everything that he eats or drinks.

Bishop Robert South (1676 – 1734)

English churchman

Sermon XVIII

Sermons Preached Upon Several Occasions Vol V (1727)

#church #England #faith #heaven #sermon #sustenance

He's a young plant, in his first year of bearing;

But his friend swears, he will be worth the rearing.

His gloss is still upon him; though 'tis true

He's yet unripe, yet take him for the blue.

You think an apricot half green is best;

There's sweet and sour, and one side good at least.

Mangos and limes, whose nourishment is little,

Though not for food, are yet preserved for pickle,

So this green writer may pretend, at least,

To whet your stomachs for a better feast.

John Dryden (1631 – 1700)

English poet, literary critic, playwright

'A Prologue'

Examen Poeticum (1693)

#adolescence #England #fruit #poetry #sonnet

"The White Lily." Robert John Thornton (circa 1768-1837)

Lillies.

The use of Oyle of Lillies.

Oyle of *Lillies* is good to supple, mollifie, and stretch sinews that be shrunk, it is good to annoynt the sides and veines in the fits of the *Stone*.

To Candy all kinde of Flowers as they grow,

with their stalks on.

Take the Flowers, and cut the stalks somewhat short, then take one pound of the whitest and hardest *Sugar* you can get, put to it eight spoonfulls of *Rose* water, and boyle it till it will roule between your fingers and your thumb, then take it from the fire, coole it with a stick, and as it waxeth cold, dip in all your Flowers, and taking them out againe suddenly, lay them one by one on the bottome of a Sive; then turne a joyned stoole with the feet upwards, set the sive on the feet thereof, cover it with a faire linnen cloath, and set a chafin-dish of coales in the middest of the stoole underneath the five, and the heat thereof will run up to the sive, and dry your Candy presently; then box them up, and they will keep all the year, and look very pleasantly.

To make the Rock Candies

upon all Spices, Flowers, and Roots.

Take two pound of *Barbary Sugar*, Clarifie it with a pint of water, and the whites of two *Eggs*, then boyle it in a posnet to the height of *Manus Christi*, then put it into an earthen Pipkidn[46] and therewith the things that you will Candy, as *Cinamon, Ginger, Nutmegs, Rose buds, Marigolds, Eringo[47] roots, &c.* cover it, and stop it close with clay or paste, then put it into a Still, with a leasurely fire under it, for the space of three dayes and three nights, then open the pot, and if the Candy begin to come, keep it unstopped for the space of three or four dayes more, and then leaving the Syrupe, take out the Candy, lay it on a Wyer grate, and put it in an Oven after the bread is drawne, and there let it remaine one night, and your Candy will dry. This is the best way for rock Candy, making so small a quantity.

The Candy Sucket for green Ginger, Lettice, Flowers.

Whatsoever you have Preserved, either Hearbs, Fruits, or Flowers, take them out of the Syrupe, and wash them in warm water, and dry

---

[46] Pipkin: a small earthenware or metal pot usually with a horizontal handle. (Merriam-Webster, 2018)

[47] Common name for Eryngium. (USDA)

them well, then boyle the *Sugar* to the height of Candy, for Flowers, and draw them through it, then lay them on the bottome of a Sive, dry them before the fire, and when they are enough, box them for your use. This is that the *Comfet-makers* use and call *Sucket Candy*.

Of Violets.

The use of Oyle of Violets.

Oyle of *Violets, Cammomile, Lillies, Elder flowers, Cowslips, Rue, Wormwood*, and *Mint*, are made after the same sort; Oyle of *Violets*, if it be rubbed about the Tempels of the head, doth remove the extream heat, asswageth the head Ache, provoketh sleep, and moistneth the braine; it is good against melancholly, dullnesse, and heavinesse of the spirits, and against swellings, and soares that be over-hot.

The Syrupe of Violets.

Take faire water, boyle it, scum it, and to every ounce of it so boyled and scummed, take six ounces of the blew of *Violets*, only shift them as before, nine times, and the last time take nine ounces of *Violets*, let them stand between times of shifting, 12 houres, keeping the liquor still on hot embers, that it may be milk warm, and no warmer; after the first shifting you must stamp and straine your last nine ounces of *Violets*, and put in only the juice of them, then take to every pint of this liquor thus prepared, one pound of *Sugar* finely beaten, boyle it, and keep it with stirring till the *Sugar* be all melted, which if you can, let be done before it boyle, and then boyle it up with a quick fire. This doth coole and open in a burning *Ague*, being dissolved in *Almond* milk, and taken; especially it is good for any Inflamation in Children. The Conserves are of the same effect.

The use of Conserve of Violets and Cowslips.

That of *Cowslips* doth marvelously strengthen the Braine, preserveth against Madnesse, against the decay of memory, stoppeth Head-ache, and most infirmities thereof; for *Violets* it hath the same use the Syrupe hath.

To make Paste of Violets, or any kind of Flowers.

Take your Flowers, pick them, and stamp them in an *Alablaster* morter, then steep them two howres in a sauser of *Rose*-water, after straine it, and steep a little *Gum Dragon* in the same water, then beat it to past, print it in your Moulds, and it will be of the very colour and tast of the Flowers, then gild them, and so you may have every Flower in his owne colour, and tast better for the mouth, then any printed colour.

Powder of Violets.

Take sweet *Ireos*[48] roots one ounce, red *Roses* two ounces, *Storax*[49] one ounce and a halfe, *Cloves* two drams, *Marjerome*[50] one dram, *Lavinder* flowers one dram and a halfe, make these into powder; then take eight graines of fine *Muske*[51] powdered, also put to it two ounces of *Rose*-water, stir them together, and put all the rest to them, and stir them halfe an hour, till the water be dryed, then set it by one day, and dry it by the fire halfe an houre, and when it is dry put it up into bagges.

Anonymous
17th Cooking and Medicinal Book
A Book of Fruits and Flowers (1653)
#England #fruits #flowers #medicine #recipes

---

[48] Iris.
[49] a tropical or subtropical tree or shrub with showy white flowers in drooping clusters.
[50] Marjoram
[51] A kind of plant juice. (Wikitionary) (Author: possible fruit include muskmelon, muscadine grape.)

Gardeners are the ultimate mixologists.

Amy Stewart (ca. 1970)

American author

The Drunken Botanist: The Plants That Create the World's Great Drinks (2013)

#botany #cocktails #liquor #UnitedStates #wine

Aquavit has its origin in Scandinavia, where it has been produced since the 15th century. The word *Aquavit* is derived from the Latin aqua vitae, "water of life". *Akvavit* gets its distinctive flavor from various spices and herbs, with the main spices being caraway and dill. It's an important part of Scandinavian drinking culture, where it is often drunk chilled and slowly sipped from a small shot glass during festive gatherings, such as Christmas dinners and weddings, and as an aperitif.

Promotional product description

Schnapsleiche Spirits (2016)

#herbs #holidays #liquor #Scandanavia #UnitedStates #water

The red Pavie of Pompone[52], or the Monstrous Pavie is monstrous indeed, that is to say, it is prodigiously large, being sometimes thirteen or fourteen Inches about, and of the * loveliest red colour in the World; and in earnest, nothing is so delightful to behold, as to see a good handsome quantity of them upon a goodly Wall Tree[53]. It is a sight that almost dazles the Eyes, and when besides all these other advantages, they come to ripen well, and in fair weather, a Garden is much honoured in being adorned with them, a Hand well satisfyed to hold them, and a Mouth most exquisitely pleased in eating them.

Jean de La Quintinie (1626 -1688)
French horticulturist
THE Compleat Gard'ner; OR, Directions for CULTIVATING AND Right ORDERING OF Fruit-GARDENS AND Kitchen-Gardens; With Divers REFLECTIONS On several Parts OF HUSBANDRY (1693)
#agronomy #France #fruit #kitchengardens #orchard

---

[52] French variety of a downy peach.
[53] Espalier

Apelles gave us supper as if he had butchered a garden, thinking he was feeding sheep and not friends. There were radishes, chicory, fenugreek[54], lettuces, leeks, onions, basil, mint, rue, and asparagus. I was afraid that after all these things he would serve me with hay, so when I had eaten some half-soaked lupins I went off.

Ammianus (ca. 2nd Cent.)
Greek writer
The Greek Anthology, Volume IV, Book XI:
"The Convivial and Satirical Epigrams" (early 10th century)
#friends #Greece #meals #supper #vegetarianism

When my vine was laden with grapes, my friends were many; when the grapes were finished, my friends disappeared.

John Wortabet, M. D. (1827 - 1908)
Scottish minister, medical doctor, linguist
Wisdom of the East, Arabian Wisdom
Selections and Translations from the Arabic (1907)
#Arabia #fruit #MiddleEast #Scotland #vineyards #wine

---

[54] A white-flowered herbaceous plant of the pea family, with aromatic seeds that are used for flavoring, especially ground and used in curry powder. (Oxford, 2019)

Ode on a Jar of Pickles.

I.

A sweet, acidulous, down-reaching thrill

Pervades my sense: I seem to see or hear

The lushy garden-grounds of Greenwich Hill

In autumn, when the crispy leaves are sere[55]:

And odours haunt me of remotest spice

From the Levant or musky-aired Cathay,

Or from the saffron-fields of Jericho,

Where everything is nice:

The more I sniff, the more I swoon away,

And what else mortal palate craves, forgo.

II.

Odours unsmelled are keen, but those I smell

Are keener; wherefore let me sniff again!

Enticing walnuts, I have known ye well

In youth, when pickles were a passing pain;

---

[55] Dry or withered. (especially of vegetation) (Oxford, 2017)

Unwitting youth, that craves the candy stem,

And sugar-plums to olives doth prefer,

And even licks the pots of marmalade

When sweetness clings to them:

But now I dream of ambergris and myrrh,

Tasting these walnuts in the poplar shade.

III.

Lo! hoarded coolness in the heart of noon,

Plucked with its dew, the cucumber is here,

As to the Dryad's parching lips a boon,

And crescent bean-pods, unto Bacchus dear;

And, last of all, the pepper's pungent globe,

The scarlet dwelling of the sylph of fire,

Provoking purple draughts; and, surfeited,

I cast my trailing robe

O'er my pale feet, touch up my tuneless lyre,

And twist the Delphic wreath to suit my head.

IV.

Here shall my tongue in other wise be soured

Than fretful men's in parched and palsied days;

And, by the mid-May's dusky leaves embowered,

Forget the fruitful blame, the scanty praise.

No sweets to them who sweet themselves were born,

Whose natures ooze with lucent saccharine;

Who, with sad repetition soothly cloyed,

The lemon-tinted morn

Enjoy, and find acetic twilight fine:

Wake I, or sleep? The pickle-jar is void.

Bayard Taylor (1825 – 1878)
American poet, literary critic, travel author, diplomat
"Ode on a Jar of Pickles"
The Atlantic Monthly (February 1872)
#poetry #UnitedStates #vegetables

Porträtt, Rudolf II som Vertumnus (c. 1590)

Guiseppe Arcimboldo (1527 – 1593).

Angelo Orders His Dinner

I, Angelo, obese, black–garmented,

Respectable, much in demand, well fed

With mine own larder's dainties, where, indeed,

Such cakes of myrrh or fine alyssum seed,

Thin as a mallow–leaf, embrowned o' the top.

Which, cracking, lets the ropy, trickling drop

Of sweetness touch your tongue, or potted nests

Which my recondite recipe invests

With cold conglomerate tidbits—ah, the bill!

(You say), but given it were mine to fill

My chests, the case so put were yours, we'll say

(This counter, here, your post, as mine to–day),

And you've an eye to luxuries, what harm

In smoothing down your palate with the charm

Yourself concocted? There we issue take;

And see! as thus across the rim I break

This puffy paunch of glazed embroidered cake,

So breaks, through use, the lust of watering chaps

And craveth plainness: do I so?

Perhaps; But that's my secret. Find me such a man

As Lippo yonder, built upon the plan

Of heavy storage, double–navelled, fat

From his own giblet's oils, an Ararat

Uplift o'er water, sucking rosy draughts

From Noah's vineyard,—crisp, enticing wafts

Yon kitchen now emits, which to your sense

Somewhat abate the fear of old events,

Qualms to the stomach,—I, you see, am slow

Unnecessary duties to forego,—

You understand? A venison haunch, haul gout.

Ducks that in Cimbrian olives mildly stew.

And sprigs of anise, might one's teeth provoke

To taste, and so we wear the complex yoke

Just as it suits,—my liking, I confess,

More to receive, and to partake no less

Still more obese, while through thick adipose

Sensation shoots, from testing tongue to toes

Far off, dim–conscious, at the body's verge,

Where the froth–whispers of its waves emerge

On the untasting sand.

Stay, now! a seat

Is bare: I, Angelo, will sit and eat.

Bayard Taylor (1825 – 1878)
American poet, literary critic, travel author, diplomat
"Angelo Orders His Dinner"
<u>The Atlantic Monthly</u> (January 1871)
#dinner #meals #poetry #restaurant #UnitedStates

Each year the big garden grew smaller and Jane - who grew flowers by choice, not corn or string beans – worked at the vegetables more than I did. Each winter I dreamed crops, dreamed marvels of canning... and each summer I largely failed. Shamefaced, I planted no garden at all.

Donald Hall (1928 – 2018)
American poet, writer, editor, critic
Life Work (1993)
#canning #dream #embarrassment #UnitedStates #work

July 13.

Being a lover of gardens, and indeed usually writing in a garden—a habit which during this rainy summer has often brought me into difficult — I have been amused by an article in the current number of London Society, entitled, 'A Revolution in Gardening'. The author, who founds his paper on the theories of a certain Mr. Robinson, concerning whom I unhappily am ignorant, is an advocate of wild gardening, and a most determined opponent of the system of 'bedding out.' He prefers dandelions to marigolds—wherein I cannot agree with him: but I grow the roots of leontodon[56], or *dent de lion*, for salad, knowing them to be both pleasant to eat and salutary.

Edward James Mortimer Collins (1827 – 1876)
English novelist, poet
Thoughts In My Garden (1880)
#England #revolution #salad #wildflowers #writers

---

[56] Leontodon is a genus of plants in the dandelion tribe within the sunflower family (Compositae), commonly known as hawkbits. (Wikipedia)

I drank at every vine.

The last was like the first.

I came upon no wine

So wonderful as thirst.

I gnawed at every root.

I ate of every plant.

I came upon no fruit

So wonderful as want.

Feed the grape and bean

To the vintner and monger:

I will lie down lean

With my thirst and my hunger.

Edna St. Vincent Millay (1892 – 1950)

American poet, playwright

'Feast'

The Harp-Weaver (1923)

#fruit #irony #poetry #UnitedStates

A Salad

O cool in the summer is salad,

And warm in the winter is love;

And a poet shall sing you a ballad

Delicious thereon and thereof.

A singer am I, if no sinner,

My muse has a marvellous wing,

And I willingly worship at dinner

The Sirens of Spring.

Take endive—like love it is bitter,

Take beet—for like love it is red;

Crisp leaf of the lettuce shall glitter,

And cress from the rivulet's bed;

Anchovies, foam–born, like the lady

Whose beauty has maddened this bard;

And olives, from groves that are shady;

And eggs—boil 'em hard.

Edward James Mortimer Collins (1827 – 1876)

English novelist, poet

The Britiish Birds, a communication from

the Ghost of Aristophanes. (1872)

#ballad #England #poetry #salad #Summer

A Discourse on Sallets[57]

26. Pudding of Carrot. Pare off some of the Crust of Manchet -Bread, and grate off half as much of the rest as there is of the Root, which must also be grated: Then take half a Pint of fresh Cream or New Milk, half a Pound of fresh Butter, six new laid Eggs (taking out three of the Whites). Mash and mingle them well with the Cream and Butter: Then put in the grated Bread and Carrots with near half a Pound of Sugar, and a little Salt; some grated Nutmeg and beaten Spices and pour all into a convenient Dish or Pan,

---

[57] Middle English spelling of salads.

buttered, to keep the Ingredients from stick-

ing and burning, set it in a quick

Oven for about an Hour, and

so have you a Composition for any

Root-Pudding.

28. Of Spinage. Take a suffici

ent Quantity of Spinach, stamp

and drain out the Juice; put to it

grated Manchet, the Yolk of as

many Eggs as in the former Com

position of the Carrot- Pudding;

some Marrow shred small, Nutmeg,

Sugar, some Corinths, (if you please)

a few Carroways, Rose, or Orange

flower Water (as you best like) to

make it grateful. Mingle all with

a little boiled Cream; and set the

Dish or Pan in the Oven,with a Gar

nish of Puff Paste. It will require

but very moderate Baking, Thus

have you Receits for Herb Puddings.

John Evelyn (1620 – 1706)

English writer, gardener, diarist

Acetaria, A Discourse on Sallets (1699)[58]

#cooking #England #recipes #vegetables

The turnip is a capricious vegetable, which seems reluctant to

show itself at its best.

Waverley Root[59] (1983 – 1982)

American journalist, author

Food: An Authoritative, Visual History and Dictionary of the Foods of the World (1986)

#UnitedStates #vegetables

---

[58] First recorded book of salads.
[59] Botanical point for horticultural name.

Circumstance

It ripen'd by the river banks,

Where, mask and moonlight aiding,

Dons Bias and Juan play their pranks,

Dark Donnas serenading.

By Moorish damsel it was pluck'd,

Beneath the golden day there ;

By swain 'twas then in London suck'd—

Who flung the peel away there.

He could not know in Pimlico,

As little she in Seville,

That it should reel upon that peel,

And—wish them at the devil.

Frederick Locker (1821–1895)
English man of letters, bibliophile, poet
London Lyrics (1857)
#England #citrus #fruit #poetry #roses

There's a bower of bean–vines in Benjamin's yard,

And the cabbages grow round it, planted for greens;

In the time of my childhood 'twas terribly hard

To bend down the bean–poles, and pick off the beans.

That bower and its products I never forget,

But oft, when my landlady presses me hard,

I think, are the cabbages growing there yet,

Are the bean–vines still bearing in Benjamin's yard?

No, the bean–vines soon withered that once used to wave,

But some beans had been gathered, the last that hung on;

And a soup was distilled in a kettle, that gave

All the fragrance of summer when summer was gone.

Thus memory draws from delight, ere it dies, An essence that

breathes of it awfully hard;

As thus good to my taste as 'twas then to my eyes,

Is that bower of bean–vines in Benjamin's yard.

Phoebe Cary (1822 - 1871)
American poet
'There's A Bower of Bean-Vines'
Poems and Parodies (1853)
#childhood #Summer #UnitedStates #vegetables

You can eat fresh tomatoes and cucumbers in a taverna with its own garden and forget there is such a thing as fast food or that if you eat too much bacon you can get cancer.

Lewis Grizzard (1946 – 1994)
American columnist, author
Chili Dogs Always Bark at Night (1989)
#cancer #comedy #diet #food #forgetfulness #UnitedStates

Think about it: Vidalia onions, which are sweet and mild, grow only in a small part of southeast Georgia.

Some have tried to duplicate the Vidalia in other parts of the country, but to no avail.

God, I am convinced, was traveling through what was to become southeast Georgia during the six days of creation and said, "Let there be a sweet, mild onion, and let it grow here and here only."

Lewis Grizzard (1946 – 1994)
American columnist, comedian, author
"Thank God, we can now preserve blessed VIdalias"
<u>Atlanta Journal Constitution</u> (August 12, 1988)
#cancer #comedy #diet #food #forgetfulness #UnitedStates

It's simply difficult to think anything but pleasant thoughts while eating a homegrown tomato.

Lewis Grizzard (1946 – 1994)
American columnist, author
<u>The Atlanta Journal</u> (June 4, 1989)
#comedy #diet #food #forgetfulness #UnitedStates

Many of the delicious soups you eat in French homes and little restaurants are made just this way, with a leek-and-potato base to which leftover vegetables or sauces and a few fresh items are added.

Simone Beck (1904 – 1991)
French cookbook author
Louisette Bertholle (1905 – 1999)
French chef, author
Julia Child (1912 – 2004)
American chef, author, television celebrity
Mastering the Art of French Cooking (1961)
#cooking #France #leftovers #soup #UnitedStates #vegetables

Ninety–nine per cent of American prunes, and 70 per cent of all the prunes in the world, are produced in California. Rising labour costs in the early 20th century resulted in one grower importing 500 monkeys to the Santa Clara Valley from Panama. Organised into gangs of 50, each with a human foreman, the monkeys were set loose into the orchards. They scampered up the trees, harvested all the plums, and ate the lot.

Molly Oldfield (b. 1979)
British author, columnist, researcher
John Mitchinson (b.1961)
British author, researcher
QI [60], *The Telegraph*, (September 10, 2012)
#fruit #labor #monkeys #orchard #Telegraph #trivia #UnitedStates

"Blowing a raspberry" comes from the Cockney rhyming slang "raspberry tart".

Molly Oldfield (b. 1979)
British author, columnist, researcher
John Mitchinson (b.1961)
British author, researcher
QI, *The Telegraph*, (September 10, 2012)
#Chile #England #fruit #slang #slur #Telegraph #trivia

---

[60] Author's note: 'Quite Interesting,' a British comedy panel game television quiz show.

"Bramble", "briar," and "broom," were once interchangeable terms for a dense, thorny thicket. The basic blackberry, *Rubus fruticosus,* hybridises very easily and more than 400 micro–species have been recorded in Britain. That's why ripening times and taste can vary so much.

Molly Oldfield (b. 1979)
British author, columnist, researcher
John Mitchinson (b.1961)
British author, researcher
QI, *The Telegraph*, (September 10, 2012)
#England #fruit #Telegraph #trivia

The first supermarket supposedly appeared on the American landscape in 1946. That is not very long ago. Until then, where was all the food? Dear folks, the food was in homes, gardens, local fields, and forests. It was near kitchens, near tables, near bedsides. It was in the pantry, the cellar, the backyard.

Joel Salatin (b. 1957)
American farmer, lecturer, author
Folks, This Ain't Normal: A Farmer's Advice for Happier Hens, Healthier People, and a Better World (2011)
#agriculture #farm #grocery #permaculture #selfsufficiency #UnitedStates

The cucumber and the tomato are both fruit; the avocado is a nut.

To assist with the dietary requirements of vegetarians, on the first

Tuesday of the month a chicken is officially a vegetable.

Jasper Fforde (b. 1961)
English novelist
Shades of Grey (2010)
#chicken #diet #England #fruit #vegetables #vegetarianism

Hence various trees their various fruits produce, some for

delightful taste, and some for use. Hence sprouting plants enrich

the plain and wood, for physic some, and some design'd fer food.

Richard Blackmore (1654 – 1729)
English physician, poet
"Creation" (1712)[61]
The Poetical Works of Richard Blackmore (1793)
#food #fruits #trees #wisdom #vegetables

---

[61] Mistakenly attributed to *"The wisdom and goodness of God in the vegetable Creation."*

Tea Kettle Topiary, Jean Collins-Pittman, Scotland

GARDENING WITH TOUCH

I'm always touching plants and vibing with them.

Gza (b. 1966)

American Rapper, Wu–Tang Clan

"Science and The Genius"

Mary Carmichael, <u>The Boston Globe</u> (Dec 3, 2011)

#vibes #UnitedStates

Touched by his hand, the wayside weed

Becomes a flower ; the lowliest reed

Beside the stream

Is clothed with beauty; gorse[62] and grass

And heather, where his footsteps pass,

The brighter seem.

Henry Wadsworth Longfellow (1807 – 1882)
American poet, educator
'Robert Burns'
The Children's Longfellow Illustrated (1908)
#poetry #Scotland #UnitedStates #walking #weeds #wildflowers

I will be the gladdest thing under the sun!

I will touch a hundred flowers

And not pick one.

Edna St. Vincent Millay (1892 – 1950)
American poet, playwright
'Afternoon on a Hill'
Renascence and Other Poems (1917)
#hiking #poetry #UnitedStates #walking #wildflowers

---

[62] A yellow-flowered shrub of the pea family, the leaves of which are modified to form spines, native to western Europe and North Africa. (Oxford, 2015)

Looke at the Feeling–plant,[63] which learned swaines

Relate to growe on the East Indian plaines,

Shrinkes up his dainty leaves if any sand

You throw thereon, or touch it with your hand.

William Browne (1591? – 1645?)
English poet
Britannia's Pastorals (1613 – 1619)
#England #poetry #sensitivity #travel

No one will understand a Japanese garden until you've walked

through one, and you hear the crunch underfoot, and you smell it,

and you experience it over time. Now there's no photograph or any

movie that can give you that experience.

J. Carter Brown (1934 – 2002)
Director Emeritus, National Gallery of Art
Academy of Achievement Interview
"Creating the Art of Culture" (May 5, 2001)
#culture #experience #Japan #photography #UnitedStates #walking

---

[63] *Mimosa pudica* , Sensitive Plant

When I touch that flower, I am not merely touching that flower. I am touching infinity. That little flower existed long before there were human beings on this earth. It will continue to exist for thousands, yes, millions of years to come.

George Washington Carver (1861 – 1943)
American scientist
First-person conversation with Glenn Clark
The Man Who Talked with the Flowers: The Intimate Life Story of Dr. George Washington Carver (1939)
#botany #science #UnitedStates #time

When I go into my garden with a spade, and dig a bed, I feel such an exhilaration and health, that I discover that I have been defrauding myself all this time in letting others do for me what I should have done with my own hands.

Ralph Waldo Emerson (1803–1882)
American essayist, poet, philosopher
Speech, January 25, 1841
"Man, the Reformer"
Nature, Addresses, and Lectures (1849).
#digging #health #nature #UnitedStates

Day after day I spent in the woods alone in order to collect my floral beauties, and put them in my little garden I had hidden in brush not far from the house, as it was considered foolishness in the neighborhood to waste time on flowers.

And many are the tears I had shed because I would break the roots or flowers of some of my pets while removing them from the ground, and strange to say all sorts of vegetation seemed to thrive under my touch until I was styled the plant doctor, and plants from all over the country would be brought to me for treatment.

George Washington Carver (1861 – 1943)
American scientist
1897 Or Thereabouts George Washington
Carver's Own Brief History of His Life (1897)
#botany #emotions #health #science #UnitedStates #wildflowers

People often... have no idea how fair the flower is to the touch, nor do they appreciate its fragrance, which is the soul of the flower.

Helen Keller (1880 – 1868)
American author, political activist, lecturer
To Love This Life: Quotations by Helen Keller (2000)
#appreciation #awareness #gratitude #soul #UnitedStates

The worst headache for the co–operative was the work of pruning the cotton plants. Usually this light work could have been done very well by women members. Unfortunately, even young women with clever hands also made mistakes. They either cut off the branches with cotton bolls or left intact the poor branches or those without bolls at all. The plants were very poorly pruned. This infuriated Wang Yunsheng who said: "This is destroying cotton!" A group of women co–operative members surrounded him and said: "Section Head, how should the work be done? Tell us! Please tell us."

Mao Tse-Tung (1893 – 1976)
Chinese revolutionary, Founder of Communism Party
"Socialist Upsurge in the Countryside" (1957)
#China #Communism #cooperatives #pruning #work

And lilies white, prepared to touch

The whitest thought, nor soil it much,

Of dreamer turned to lover.

Elizabeth Barrett Browning (1806 – 1861)
English poet
"A Flower in a Letter" (1856)
#dream #England #love #poetry #soil

And lilies are still lilies, pulled

By smutty hands, though spotted from their white.

Elizabeth Barrett Browning (1806 – 1861)

English poet

Aurora Leigh (1856)

#dirt #England #novel #poetry #soil

Gardening gloves are for sissies. I always have dirt under my nails.

Hilarie Burton (b. 1982)

American actress

"Esquire Presents Me in My Place with Hilarie Burton" (June 6, 2011)

#actress #dirt #gloves #Hollywood #nails #United States

I collapse

I touch myself

a flower's gesture

frail

cold.

Alejandra Pizarnik (1936 – 1972)

Argentinian poet

The Galloping Hour: French Poems (2018)

#Argentina #France #frailty #poetry

'Green fingers' are a fact, and a mystery only to the unpracticed. But green fingers are the extensions of a verdant heart. A good garden cannot be made by somebody who has not developed the capacity to know and love growing things.

Russell Page (1906 – 1985)
British designer
The Education of the Gardener (1962)
#England #green #love #mystery

When Charlotte Moss needs to decompress, the Manhattan–based interior designer nips out to her garden in East Hampton, New York, and starts clipping. "I love the architecture of trees, that you can train them how to grow," says the author of seven books about style and decor. "It's all about control: When you feel like your life is getting out of hand, just go clip your topiary!"

Charlotte Moss[64] (ca.1960)
American interior designer and author
"Charlotte Moss's New Textile Collection"
Architectural Digest (December 2011)
#architecture #control #pruning #topiary #UnitedStates

---

[64] Botanical point for horticultural name.

Touching a flower is touching life; touching the sun is touching life; touching the skin, touching the sand, all of this means touching life! No touch, no life!

Mehmet Murat ildan (b. 1965)
Turkish playwright, novelist, philosopher
"Murat ildan Quotations" (2010)
#adages #life #Turkey

Sheila O'Monahan: "Please do sit down at your age, gentlemen. I'll sit, I'll sit [looking around the room] I'll sit on that little stoolie and we'll try to get over the hedge."

Judge James Trumbull: "Get over the hedge?"

Sheila O'Monahan: "Grandda always said there was a hedge standing between people who are strangers; one to the other, until they talked back and forth."

Sheila O'Monahqn (Margaret O'Brian)
Judge James Trumbull (Lewis Stone)
Edward Buzzell (1895 – 1985)
American director, Metro–Goldwyn–Mayer
"Three Wise Fools" (1946)
#Hollywood #movies #pruning #UnitedState

It was such a pleasure to sink one's hands into the warm earth, to feel at one's fingertips the possibilities of the new season.

Kate Morton (b. 1976)
Australian author
The Forgotten Garden (2008)
#Australia #digging #hands #season #soil

Stiefel, in his inspired state, ventured upon exploits which were all but impossible. He placed his left arm under his right, and thus supporting its weight and that of its plush sleeve, in a horizontal position, snuffed the candle before the whole company, and did it rather skillfully on the whole; somewhat like a gardener on a ladder holding out his pruning shears at arm's length to a high branch and snipping off the whole concern by a slight movement of his hand at the bottom.

Jean Paul Friedrich Richter (1763 - 1825)
German Romantic writer, philosopher
Siebenkäs (1796-1797)
#Germany #metaphor #novel #pruning

Pluck not the wayside flower,

It is the traveller's dower;

A thousand passers-by

Its beauties may espy,

May win a touch of blessing

From Nature's mild caressing.

The sad of heart perceives

A violet under leaves

Like sonic fresh-budding hope;

The primrose on the slope

A spot of sunshine dwells,

And cheerful message tells

Of kind renewing power;

The nodding bluebell's dye

Is drawn from happy sky.

Then spare the wayside flower!

It is the traveller's dower.

William Allingham (1824 – 1899)

Irish poet, editor

'Wayside Flowers'

Songs, Ballads, and Stories (1877)

#hiking #Ireland #nature #poetry #wildflowers

152

Fingers now scented with sage and rosemary,

a kneeling gardener is lost

in savory memories.

Dr. SunWolf (ca. 1955)
American professor, writer, poet
"WordWhispers" (after 2009)[65]
#fragrance #herbs #memories #poetry #tweet #UnitedStates

He came to his fields. He stopped in front of them. He bent down, picked up a handful of that rich earth full of air and seeds. It was an earth full of good will. He felt all its good will with his fingers.

Jean Giono (1895–1970)
French author
Regain (1930)[66]
#earth #farm #France #goodwill #literature #novel #seeds

[65] Confirmed by Dr. Sunwolf (2019)
[66] Translated from the French by Henri Fluchè and Geoffrey Myers, *Harvest,* (1939)

I know the pleasure of pulling up root vegetables. They are solvable mysteries.

Novella Carpenter (ca. 1955)
American author, journalist, urban farmer
Farm City: The Education of an Urban Farmer (2009)
#farm #mystery #urbanfarms #UnitedStates #vegetables

Man takes root at his feet, and at best he is no more than a potted plant in his house or carriage till he has established communication with the soil by the loving and magnetic touch of his soles to it.

John Burroughs (1837 – 1927)
American naturalist, essayist
Winter Sunshine (1875)
#nature #philosophy #UnitedStates #walking #Winter

Digging

Between my finger and my thumb

The squat pen rests; snug as a gun.

Under my window, a clean rasping sound

When the spade sinks into gravelly ground:

My father, digging. I look down

Till his straining rump among the flowerbeds

Bends low, comes up twenty years away

Stooping in rhythm through potato drills

Where he was digging.

The coarse boot nestled on the lug, the shaft

Against the inside knee was levered firmly.

He rooted out tall tops, buried the bright edge deep

To scatter new potatoes that we picked,

Loving their cool hardness in our hands.

By God, the old man could handle a spade.

Just like his old man.

My grandfather cut more turf in a day

Than any other man on Toner's bog.

Once I carried him milk in a bottle

Corked sloppily with paper. He straightened up

To drink it, then fell to right away

Nicking and slicing neatly, heaving sods

Over his shoulder, going down and down

For the good turf. Digging.

The cold smell of potato mould, the squelch and slap

Of soggy peat, the curt cuts of an edge

Through living roots awaken in my head.

But I've no spade to follow men like them.

Between my finger and my thumb

The squat pen rests.

I'll dig with it.

Seamus Heaney (1939 - 2013)

Irish author, playwright

"Digging"

Death of a Naturalist (1966)

#farm #Ireland #peat #poetry #turf #vegetables #writing

It's something that plant lovers have long suspected, but now Australian scientists have found evidence that plants really can *feel* when we're touching them.

Not only that, but different sensations trigger a cascade of physiological and genetic changes, depending on the stimulation the plants are receiving, whether it's a few drops of rain, or a little soft pat, which is probably the coolest thing we've heard all week.

"Although people generally assume plants don't feel when they are being touched, this shows that they are actually very sensitive to it," said lead researcher Olivier Van Aken from the University of Western Australia.

"While plants don't appear to complain when we pinch a flower, step on them or just brush by them while going for a walk, they are fully aware of this contact and are rapidly responding to our treatment of them," he added...

One thing the scientists found was that spraying water droplets on plants caused them to change the expression of thousands of genes - a dramatic physiological response that started within minutes of the stimulus and stopped within half an hour.

"We were able to show that this response was not caused by any active compounds in the spray but rather by the physical contact caused by water drops landing on the leaf surface," says Van Aken.

Curious to know how else they might respond, the team also found that gently patting the plants or touching them with tweezers could trigger a similar physiological cascade. So could a sudden shadow falling over their leaves.

All of this information could be essential to plants survival in the wild, the researchers explain in the journal Plant Physiology.

"Unlike animals, plants are unable to run away from harmful conditions. Instead, plants appear to have developed intricate stress defence systems to sense their environment and help them detect danger and respond appropriately," says Van Aken… The good news? Singing seems to be pretty safe. "As yet, there's no evidence to back the idea held by some people that the vibrations caused by just talking to plants has a strong enough effect to move plants,"

Fiona MacDonald (ca. 1977)
CEO, ScienceAlert
"Plants Really Do Respond to The Way
We Touch Them, Scientists Reveal"
Nature, ScienceAlert (May 3, 2016)
#genetics #nature #research #science

There's something satisfying about getting your hands in the soil.

Elizabeth Ann Bucchianeri (1976)

American author

Vocation of a Gadfly (2018)

#fiction #literature #Ireland #soil #UnitedStates

One touch of Nature makes all the world kin.

Ulysses

Greek Commander

William Shakespeare (1564 – 1616)

English playwright, poet, actor

"Troilus and Cressida" (ca. 1602)

#England #family #nature #play #theatre #tragedy

GARDENING WITH THE PHYSIC

What the right flower can do, with luck, is heal the gardener,

making him fit (more or less) to love, by steps however slow.

Growing old, still in awe, still sitting at her feet.

Henry Clay Mitchell (1923–1993)
American columnist, author
The Essential Earthman: Henry Mitchell on Gardening (1998)
#aging #healing #health #UnitedStates #walking

By him, whom you have learned to love; learn how to be cured;
for you, the same hand shall cause the wound and the remedy.
The earth nourishes wholesome plants, and the same produces
injurious ones; and full oft is the nettle the neighbour of the rose.

Publius Ovidius Naso[67] **(43 BC – 17/18 AD)**
Roman poet
The Heroïdes, Or Epistles of the Heroines;
The Amours ; Art of Love and minor works (ca. 5 BC)
#healing #Italy #love #poetry #Rome

Contra vim mortis non crescit herba in hortiss, Latin: "No herb
grows in the gardens against the power of death", is a phrase
which appears in medieval literature. According to Jan
Wielewicki in his *Dziennik spraw Domu zakonnego OO.
Jezuitów u św. Barbary w Krakowie* these words were said by
Sigismund III Vasa on his deathbed. In *Das Buch der Zitate* by
Gerhard Hellwig the phrase appears in *Flos medicinae*.[68]

Commonly attributed to **St. John the Good (c. 641 – 649)**
Catholic Archbishop of Milan
<u>World Heritage Encyclopedia Edition</u> (2017)
#Catholicism #death #herbs #Italy #Latin #literature #medieval

---

[67] Commonly known as Ovid
[68] Also known as *Regimen sanitatis Salernitanum.* (ca. 11th – 13th century)

Fix'd like a Plant on his peculiar Spot,

To draw nutrition, propagate and rot.

Alexander Pope (1688 - 1744)
English poet
"An Essay on Man. In Epistles to a Friend" Epistle II (1733)
#England #growth #life #nutrition

The name Salvia "*salviya*" derives from the Latin *salvere* ("to feel well and healthy, health, heal"), the verb related to salus (health, well-being, prosperity or salvation); referring to the herb's healing properties. Pliny the Elder was the first author known to describe a plant called "Salvia" by the Romans, likely describing the type species for the genus Salvia, Salvia officinalis.

Gaius Plinius Secundus (23 A.D. – 79 A.D.)[69]
Roman author, naturalist, natural philosopher,
Naval and army commander of the early Roman Empire
Pliny's Natural History (77 A.D.)
Encyclopedia Britannica (1911)
#botany #herbs #Italy #nature #Rome

---

[69] Author's note: Commonly known as Pliny the Elder.

Generally regarded as identical with the Teucrium Marum of Linnæus, a sweet-smelling shrub found in the south of Europe and the East, by us commonly known as "herb mastich," somewhat similar to marjoram. Fée says that the marum of Egypt is a kind of sage, the *Salvia Æthiopis* of Linnæus.

Gaius Plinius Secundus (23 A.D. – 79 A.D.)
Roman author, naturalist, natural philosopher
Naval and army commander of the early Roman Empire
Pliny's Natural History (77 A.D.)
Encyclopedia Britannica (1911)
#botany #Egypt #herbs #Italy #nature #Rome

Gardening is a labour full of tranquility and satisfaction; natural and instructive, and as such contributes the most serious, contemplation, experience, health, and longevity.

John Evelyn (1620 – 1706)
English writer, gardener, diarist
Directions for the Gardiner and other Horticultural Advice (1666, 1932)
#contributions #England #health #peace #satisfaction

According to an early tradition, black hellebore administered by the soothsayer and physician Melampus (whence its name *Melampodium*), was the means of curing the madness of the daughters of Proetus, king of Argos. The drug was used by the ancients in paralysis, gout and other diseases, more particularly in insanity, a fact frequently alluded to by classical writers, *e.g.* Horace (*Sat.* ii. 3. 80-83, *Ep. ad Pis.* 300). Various superstitions were in olden times connected with the cutting of black hellebore. The best is said by Pliny (*Nat. hist.* xxv. 21) to grow on Mt Helicon. Of the three Anticyras that in Phocis was the most famed for its hellebore, which, being there used combined with "sesamoides[70]," was, according to Pliny, taken with more safety than elsewhere.

Gaius Plinius Secundus (23 A.D. – 79 A.D.)
Roman author, naturalist, natural philosopher,
Naval and army commander of the early Roman Empire
Pliny's Natural History (77 A.D.)
Encyclopedia Britannica (1911)
#drugs #Greece #insanity #medicine #superstitions #UnitedStates

---

[70] Sesamoiditis is the inflammation of the sesamoid bones, along with the surrounding tissues. (Sesamoiditis.org, 2019)

A walk in the garden once a–day is exercise, enough for any thinking being.

Sir Walter Scott (1771 – 1832)
Scottish novelist, poet, playwright, historian.
The Antiquary (1816)
#exercise #history #life #Scotland #walking

Do not go to the garden of flowers!

O Friend! Go not there;

 In your body is the garden of flowers.

Take your seat on the thousand petals of the lotus,

 And there gaze on the Infinite Beauty.

Kabir (c.1440 – 1518)
Indian mystic, saint
Songs of Kabîr (15th century)
#beauty #health #India #mysticism #poetry

The garden is the poor man's apothecary.

Traditional German Proverb
#drugs #Germany #herbs #pharmacy #proverbs

Did the world produce more men equal in assiduity and unwearied research, it would be adorned by more of equal distinction : so true is it — a fact important to all men, but, which ought, in a more especial manner, to be zealously inculcated on the minds of youth—that industry is not only one of the parents of knowledge, but an essential component of human greatness. Without this most important of qualities, an intellect of the highest order but resembles a tract of fertile soil defectively cultivated, shooting forth a few luxuriant plants, but overrun with weeds, and not exempt from poisonous productions; while with it, minds much less richly endowed by nature, are converted into gardens abounding in all that is ornamental and useful.

Joseph Delaplaine (1777–1824)
American publisher
Delaplaine's repository of the lives and portraits of distinguished American characters (1815)
#intelligence #industry #labor #UnitedStates #weeds #youth

There are two types of onions, the big white Spanish and the little red Italian. The Spanish has more food value and is therefore chosen to make soup for huntsmen and drunkards, two classes of people who require fast recuperation.

Alexandre Dumas (1802–1870)
French novelist, playwright
Le Grand Dictionaire de Cuisine (1873)
#cookbook #food #France #recipes #recuperation #soup

Onions do promote a man to veneryous[71] actes, and to somnolence.

Andrew Boorde (1490 – 1549)
English traveler, physician, writer
The fyrst boke of the introduction of knowledge
or, A dyetary of helth (1542)
#diet #England #health #lust #sleep

One of the most important resources that a garden makes available for use, is the gardener's own body. A garden gives the body the dignity of working in its own support. It is a way of rejoining the human race.

Wendell Berry (b. 1934)
American novelist, poet, essayist, farmer
"The Reactor and the Garden" (1979)
The Gift of Good Land (2009)
#agriculture #dignity #humanity #resources #UnitedStates

---

[71] Venereous: of or relating to sexual pleasure or indulgence. (Merriam-Webster, 2019)

A Powder That has Restored Sight When Almost Lost

Take of betony, celandine, saxifrage, eye–bright[72], pennyroyal, and levisticum[73] of each one handful; of aniseseeds and cinnamon of each half an ounce; take also of grains of paradise, ginger, hyssop, parsley, origany[74], osier of the mountain[75], of each one dram; galangal[76] and sugar, of each one ounce; make all into a fine powder, and eat of it every day with your meat such a quantity as you used to eat of salt, and instead of salt–osier, you must have that at the Physic Garden.

Eliza Smith (ca. 1682 – 1732)
American housekeeper, cookbook author
The Compleat Housewife,
or Accomplished Gentlewoman's Companion (1727)
#herbs #medicine #recipe #sight #UnitedStates

---

[72] A small plant of the figwort family with flowers resembling snapdragons. Found in dry fields and along roadsides, it was formerly used as a remedy for eye problems. (Oxford, 2012)

[73] Lovage.

[74] Oregano.

[75] 'Osier of the mountain' could be either the willow, *Salix,* or red dogwood, *Cornus* species.

[76] An Asian plant of the ginger family, the aromatic rhizome of which is widely used in cooking and herbal medicine. (Oxford, 2012)

The root of all health is in the brain. The trunk of it is in emotion. The branches and leaves are the body. The flower of health blooms when all parts work together.

Traditional Kurdish Saying

#botany #health #Kurdistan

Our land passes in and out of our bodies just as our bodies pass

in and out of our land.

Wendell Berry (b. 1934)

American novelist, poet, essayist, farmer

The Unsettling of America: Culture & Agriculture (2015)

#agriculture #compost #land #UnitedStates

Gardening requires lots of water — most of it in the form of

perspiration.

Louis Bernard Erickson (1913-1990)

American editorial cartoonist, illustrator

The Atlanta Journal (1951 - 1982)

#exercise #humor #labor #sweat #UnitedStates

What a man needs in gardening is a cast–iron back, with a hinge in it.

Charles Dudley Warner (1829 – 1900)

American essayist, author

My Summer in a Garden (1871)

#responsibility #UnitedStates #warning

Our bodies are our gardens, to the which our wills are gardeners. So that if we will plant nettles or sow lettuce, set hyssop and weed up thyme, supply it with one gender of herbs or distract it with many—either to have it sterile with idleness, or manured with industry—why, the power and corrigible authority of this lies in our wills.

Iago, character
William Shakespeare (1564 – 1616)
English playwright, poet, actor
"Othello" (1603)
#England #medicine #play #poison #theatre

Vis medicatrix naturae.[77]

Nature is the best physician of diseases.

Attributed to Hippocrates (c. 460 – c. 370 BC)
No known origination
#disease #doctor #Greece #Latin #medicine #nature

---

[77] Latin translation for the Greek phrase, νόσων φύσεις ἰητροί.

Within the infant rind of this small flower

Poison hath residence and medicine power.

For this, being smelt, with that part cheers each part;

Being tasted, stays all senses with the heart.

Two such opposèd kings encamp them still,

In man as well as herbs—grace and rude will.

And where the worser is predominant,

Full soon the canker death eats up that plant.

Romeo, character
William Shakespeare (1564 – 1616)
English playwright, poet, actor
"Romeo and Juliet" (1597)
#England #medicine #play #poison #theatre

Gardening is the most therapeutic and defiant act you can do,

especially in the inner city, you get strawberries.

Ron Finley (ca. 1956)
American fashion designer, "Gangsta Gardener",
proponent of urban gardening
"guerilla gardening in south central LA" at TED2013 (2013)
#defiance #design #fruit #therapy #UnitedStates

The word herb is derived from the old French *erbe* and, from its first appearance in English in the late 13th century, meant both a plant without a woody stem and a plant of particular medicinal or culinary value. The "h" first appeared in the 15th century but wasn't voiced until the 19th century (which is why Americans still refer to "erbs"). Any plant with officinalis in its Latin name can be used as a medicine.

In 1571, when smoking was first introduced to Europe from the New World, the Spanish doctor Nicolás Monardes established tobacco's reputation as a cure for more than 20 ailments, including cancer.

Molly Oldfield (b. 1979)
British author, columnist, researcher
John Mitchinson (b.1961)
British author, researcher
QI, The Telegraph (March 6, 2013)
#cure #England #herbs #smoking #Telegraph #tobacco #trivia

I really think the pure passion for flowers, the only one which long sickness leaves untouched with its chilling influence. Often, during this weary illness of mine, have I looked upon new books with perfect apathy, when if a friend has sent me but a few flowers, my heart has leaped up to their dreamy hues and odors, with a sudden sense of renovated childhood, which seems one of the mysteries of our being.

Felicia Dorothea Browne Hemans (1793 – 1835)
English poet
"Mrs.Hemans To Mrs. Lawrence from Redesdale, near Dublin" (1835)
The Last Autumn at a Favorite Residence, with other poems:
and recollections (1836)
#childhood #England #flowers #Ireland #passion #sickness

One of the healthiest ways to gamble is with a spade and a package of garden seeds.

Dan Bennett (b. 1962)
American comedian, juggler
Comedy routine (ca.1990's)
#gambling #humor #seeds #tools #UnitedStates

Gardening, which is a modification of walking, offers many advantages both to the delicate and the strong, and it is a species of exercise which we can adjust to our powers. In a continued walk you must go on—you must return; there is no appeal, even if you have gone too far, and would willingly give up any further exertion. But, while gardening, you are still at home—your exertions are devoted to objects the most interesting, because progressive; hope and faith form a part of your stimulus. The happy future, when flowers shall bloom around you, supersedes in your thoughts the vexatious present or the mournful past. About you are the budding treasures of spring, or the gorgeous productions of summer, or the rich hues of those beauties which autumn pours forth most lavishly before it departs,—and is succeeded by winter. Above you are the gay warblers, who seem to hail you as you mingle in the sylvan scenes which are not all theirs, but which you share and appropriate. The ruffled temper, the harassed mind, may find a solace in the occupation of gardening, which aids the effect of exercise and the benign influence of fresh air. Stores of future and never–dying interest are buried in the earth with every seed, only to spring up again redoubled in their value. A lady, as a writer in the 'Quarterly Review' observes, should 'not only have but know her plants.' And her enjoyment of those delights is truly enhanced by that personal care, without which few gardens, however superintended by the scientific gardener, can prosper, and which bless as they thrive; her plants bestow health on the frame which is bowed down to train them—they give to her the blessing of a calm and rational pleasure—they relieve her from the necessity of excitement—they promote alike, in the wealthy and the poor, these gentle exertions which are coupled with the most poetical and the sweetest of associations.

Florence Hartley (ca. 19th century)

American writer

The Ladies Book of Etiquette and Manual of Politeness: a complete handbook for the use of the lady in polite society (1860)

#exercise #manners #seasons #UnitedStates #walking

Gardening is the greatest tonic and therapy a human being can have. Even if you have only a tiny piece of earth, you can create something beautiful, which we all have a great need for. If we begin by respecting plants, it's inevitable we'll respect people.

Audrey Hepburn (1929 – 1993)
English actress
Audrey Hepburn: An Intimate Portrait (1993)
#beauty #England #Hollywood #land #respect #therapy

Loving the wind that bent me. All my hurts

My garden-spade can heal. A woodland walk,

A wild rose, or rock-loving columbine,

Salve my worst wounds, and leave no cicatrice.

Ralph Waldo Emerson (1803 – 1882)
American essayist, lecturer, philosopher, poet
"Musketaquid"
Poems (1847)
#healing #health #poetry #UnitedStates #walking

William Blake (1757- 1827)

English poet, painter, printmaker.

The Sick Rose (1794)

Songs of Experience (1825)

#England #humanity #metaphor #poetry #sickness

George III is well known in children's history books for being the "mad king who lost America". In recent years, though, it has become fashionable among historians to put his "madness" down to the physical, genetic blood disorder called porphyria. Its symptoms include aches and pains, as well as blue urine…

However, a new research project based at St George's, University of London, has concluded that George III did actually suffer from mental illness after all… The researchers have even thrown doubt on one of the key planks in the case for porphyria, the blue urine. George III's medical records show that the king was given medicine based on gentian. This plant, with its deep blue flowers, is still used today as a mild tonic, but may turn the urine blue.

So maybe it wasn't the king's "madness" that caused his most famous symptom. It could have simply been his medicine.

Lucy Worsley (b. 1972)
English historian
BBC News Magazine, "Fit To Rule" (April 15, 2013)
#BBC #England #GreatBritain #history #king #madness #royalty

If you really want to draw close to your garden, you must remember first of all that you are dealing with a being that lives and dies; like the human body, with its poor flesh, its illnesses at times repugnant. One must not always see it dressed up for a ball, manicured and immaculate.

Fernand Lequenne (1906 – 19__)
French writer
Mon ami le jardin (1941)[78]
#France #health #human #living

Human beings and plants have co-evolved for millions of years, so it makes perfect sense that our complex bodies would be adapted to absorb needed, beneficial compounds from complex plants and ignore the rest.

Dr. Andrew Weil (b. 1942)
American physician, author
"Why Plants Are (Usually) Better Than Drugs"
"The Blog"
The Huffington Post (January 19, 2010)
#drugs #evolution #humanity #UnitedStates

---

[78] My Friend The Garden.

GARDENING WITH SAGE
~ Otherwise known as Common Sense ~

Le bon goût est la fleur du bon sens.

Good taste is the flower of good sense.

Achilles Poincelot (1822 – fl. 1850)

French philosopher, author

Étude de l' Homme ou Reflexions Morales (1846)[79]

#Italy #intelligence #morals #sensitivity #style #wisdom

---

[79] English translation: *Studies of Man or Moral Reflections.*

Proverbs are potted wisdom.

Charles Buxton (1822 – 1871)
English philanthropist, politician
Notes of Thought (1883)
#adagess #England #proverbs #wisdom

Transplanting is part of a garden's good discipline.

George Washington Cable (1844 – 1925)
American author
The Amateur Garden (1914)
#discipline #maintenance #transplanting #UnitedStates

You were made for enjoyment, and the world was filled with things which you will enjoy, unless you are too proud to be pleased with them, or too grasping to care for what you cannot turn to other account than mere delight. Remember that the most beautiful things in the world are the most useless: peacocks and lilies, for instance.

John Ruskin (1819 – 1900)
English art critic
The Stones of Venice (1851 – 1853)
#beauty #delight #England #enjoyment #pride #usefulness

Oh, my heart, if thou desirest ease in this life, keep thy secrets undisclosed like the modest rose-bud. Take warning from that lovely flower, which, by expanding its hitherto hidden beauties when in full bloom, gives its leaves and its happiness to the winds.

Unnamed Persian poet
Sir Gore Ouseley (1770 – 1844)
English entrepreneur, diplomat, orientalist
Biographical notices of Persian poets;
with critical and explanatory remarks (1846)
#England #Iran #Persia #secrets #warning

Virtues, like plants, reward the attention bestowed upon them by growing more and more thrifty.

Christian Nevell Bovee (1820 – 1904)
American author
Intuitions and Summaries of Thoughts (1862)
#adagess #attention #thrift #UnitedStates #virtue

Love your neighbor, yet pull not down your hedge.

George Herbert (1593 – 1633)
English Poet, priest, theologian, orator
Jacula prudentum, or, Outlandish proverbs, sentences &c. (1651)
#England #neighbors #proverbs #wisdom

On every thorn delightful wisdom grows; In every rill a sweet instruction flows.

Edward Young (1683 -1765)
English poet, critic, philosopher, theologian
The Universal Passion (1725)
#adages #England #instruction #wisdom

Cultivate poverty like a garden herb, like sage. Do not trouble yourself much to get new things, whether clothes or friends. Turn the old; return to them. Things do not change; we change. Sell your clothes and keep your thoughts. God will see that you do not want society.

Henry David Thoreau (1817 – 1862)
American essayist, poet, and philosopher
Walden; or, Life in the Woods (1854)
#herbs #humility #society #thrift #UnitedStates

The most beautiful garden is always the one that we have made it with our own efforts!

Mehmet Murat ildan (b. 1965)
Turkish playwright, novelist, philosopher
"Muratildan Quotations" (2010)
#adages #beauty #effort #labor #Turkey #wisdom

The real wealth of a good gardener is not his salary but the marvelous flowers he is raising in the garden!

Mehmet Murat ildan (b. 1965)
Turkish playwright, novelist, philosopher
"Muratildan Quotations" (2010)
#adages #Turkey #wealth #wisdom

The best side of a character is developed by him who commends it, as grapes grow on the sweetest side of the cluster facing the sun.

Christian Nevell Bovee (1820 – 1904}
American author
Intuitions and summaries of thoughts (1862)
#character #fruit #UnitedStates #sunshine

The Gardener and the Bear

In the eastern part of Persia there lived at one time a gardener whose one joy in life was his flowers and fruit trees. He had neither wife, nor children, nor friends; nothing except his garden. At length, however, the good man wearied of having no one to talk to. He decided to go out into the world and find a friend. Scarcely was he outside the garden before he came face to face with a bear, who, like the gardener, was looking for a companion. Immediately a great friendship sprang up between these two.

The gardener invited the bear to come into his garden, and fed him on quinces and melons. In return for this kindness, when the gardener lay down to take his afternoon nap, the bear stood by and drove off the flies.

One afternoon it happened that an unusually large fly alighted on the gardener's nose. The bear drove it off, but it only flew to the gardener's chin. Again the bear drove it away, but in a few moments it was back once more on the gardener's nose. The bear now was filled with rage. With no thought beyond that of punishing the fly, he seized a huge stone, and hurled it with such force at the gardener's nose that he killed not only the fly, but the sleeping gardener.

It is better to have a wise enemy than a foolish friend.

Bidpai (ca. 100 BC)
Legendary Sanskrit sage
Panchatantra (ca. 100 BC – 500 AD)
#bear #fable #Iran #Persia

You can't get up too early, if you have a garden.

Charles Dudley Warner (1829 – 1900)
American essayist, author
My Summer in a Garden (1871)
#adagess #discipline #morning #proverbs #UnitedStates

A garden is an awful responsibility. You never know what you may be aiding to grow in it.

Charles Dudley Warner (1829 – 1900)
American essayist, author
My Summer in a Garden (1871)
#responsibility #UnitedStates #warning

Gnomologia

Many things grow in the garden that were never sown there.

A low hedge is easily leap'd over.

A myrtle among thorns is a myrtle still.

A shroved tree may stand long.

A thin meadow is soon mowed.

A Thistle is a fat sallad for an ass's mouth.

A Tree is better known by its Fruit than by its Leaves.

A young Twig is easier twisted than an old Tree.

All Flowers are not one Garland.

As is the Gardener, so is the Garden.

As welcome as Flowers in May.

Better to be stung by a Nettle, than prick'd by a Rose.

Beauty in Women is like the Flowers in the Spring; But Virtue

is like the Stars in Heaven.

Beauty may have fair Leaves, yet bitter Fruit.

Best to Bend it while a Twig.

Black Plums may eat as sweet as white.

Corn in good years is Hay; in ill years Straw is Corn.

Deeds is Fruits, Words are Leaves.

Fruit ripens not well in the Shade.

Good nature is the proper Soil upon which Virtue grows.

Great Trees keep under the little ones.

He had been out Hawking for Butterflies.

He that plants Trees, loves others beside himself.

He that scatters Thorns, must not walk Barefoot.

He that sows in the Highway, tires his Oxen',

and loseth his Corn.

He that would have Fruit, must climb the Tree.

He useth the Rake, more than the Fork.

He who plants a Walnut–Tree, expects not to eat of the Fruit.

If you lie upon Roses when young,

you'll lie upon Thorns when old.

It is bad Soil, where no Flowers will grow.

It is a bad Stake, that will not stand in the Hedge one Year.

It is the finest Flower in his Garden.

Like the Gardener's dog; that neither eats Cabbage himself nor

allows any one else.

Like Lips, like Lettuce.

Lilies are whitest in a BlackMoor's hand.

Love thy Neighbor, but cut not up thy Hedge for him.

Many rise under their Burthens[80] more like Camels

than Palm–trees.

Many Stroaks[81] fell the Oak.

Many Things grow in the Garden, that were never sow'd there.

Money, like Dung, does no Good till tis' spread.

Nip the Briar in the Bud.

No Autumn–Fruit, without Spring–Blossoms.

No body is fond of fading Flowers.

No Pear without a Stalk.

No Rose without a Prickle.

Noble Plants suit not with a Stubborn Soil.

Offer not the Pear, to him that gave the Apple.

Out, Nettle; in, Dock[82].

---

[80] Burdens
[81] Strokes
[82] Native plant, (*Rumex* sp.) with large thick leaves that can be rubbed on skin that has been stung by nettles to make it less painful. (Oxford, 2015)

Patience grows not in every Garden.

Plant the Crab–Tree where you will, it will never grow Pippens.

Plants too often removed will not thrive.

Remove an old Tree, and you'll kill it.

Roses have their Prickles.

Sow Wheat in Dirt, sow Rye in Dust.

Strait Trees have crooked Roots.

Such as the Tree, such as the Fruit.

The Boughs that bear most, hang the lowest.

The Pine wishes her self a shrub, when the Axe is at her roots.

The Sun may do its Duty, tho' your Grapes are not ripe.

Tis not the Husbandman, but the good Weather,

that makes Corn grow.

To cut down an Oak, and plant a Thistle.

Under the Flowers are Thorns.

When all Fruit fails, welcome Haws.

Where there are Reeds, there is Water.

Wholesome and Poisonous Herbs grow in the same Garden.

Would you have Potatoes grow by the Pot–side?

You ask an Elm–tree for Pears.

You set Saffron, and there came up Wolfs–bane.

What God will, no Frost can kill.

Early Sow, Early Mow.

April Showers – Bring May Flowers.[83]

If you would a good Hedge have, carry the Leaves to the Grave.

Sow Beans in the Mud, and they'll grow like Wood.

Graft good Fruit on all, or Graft not at all.

The Higher the Plumb–Tree, the riper the Plumb,

The richer the Cobler, the blacker his Thumb.

This Rule in Gardening never forget,

To sow dry, and set wet.

Collected by **Thomas Fuller (1654 – 1734)**

English churchman, historian

*Gnomologia: adagies and proverbs; wise sentences and witty sayings,
ancient and modern, foreign and British* (1732)

#adages #beauty #England #proverbs #wit

---

[83] Author: "Now you know the source."

Virtue, like a strong and hardy plant will root where it can find an ingenuous nature and a mind not averse to labor.

Plutarch (46 AD – 120 AD)
Greek biographer, essayist
Parallel Lives of Noble Grecians and Romans (100 AD)
#adages #Greece #labor #virtue #workethic

Fools are not planted or sowed, they grow of themselves.

Russian proverb

Fools grow without watering.

Italian proverb

An ill weed grows of its own accord.

French proverb

Weeds want no sowing.

English proverb

Ill weeds grow soonest and last longest.

Danish proverb

Collected by **Rev. Dwight Edwards Marvin (1851 – 1940)**
American clergyman, author
Curiosities in Proverbs (1916)
#adages #Denmark #England #France #Italy #proverbs #Russia
#UnitedStates

Take a vine of a good soil, and a daughter of a good mother.

Di buona terra tò la vigna, di buon madre tò la figlia.

Italian proverb
Collected by **Harry George Bohn** (1796 – 1884)
English publisher
A Handbook of Proverbs (1855)
#adages #daughter #England #Italy #mother #proverbs #soil

We give advice by the bucket, but take it by the grain.

William Rounseville Alger (1822 – 1905)
Unitarian minister, author
The New Era (1872)
#adages #advice #listen #proverbs #UnitedStates

Leave not the business of today to be done tomorrow, for who knoweth what may be thy condition to–morrow? The rose–garden, which today is full of flowers, when tomorrow thou wouldst pluck a rose, may not afford thee one.

Abul-Qâsem Ferdowsi Tusi (960 – 1020)
Persian poet
Collected by William Alexander Clouston (1843 – 1896)
Scottish 19th century folklorist
Book of Wise Sayings, Selected Largely from Eastern Sources (1893)
#folklore #Persia #poetry #procrastination
#regret #Scotland #wisdom

The end of the garden is at the end of the hose.

Michael Peter Garofalo (b. 1945)

American librarian, teacher, philosopher

"Pulling Onions" (1999)

#adagess #aphorism #solutions #tools #UnitedStates

END OF VOLUME III.

To the following individuals, organizations, and universities without which the original sources or use of work would not have happened.:

Kathryn Johnson, US MacMillan Publishers

Declan Taintor, Henry Holt & MacMillan Publishers

Erin Dawkins, House of Taylor

Whitney Lynn, Artist, University of Washington

Lynn Stegner

Andrea Sprott, Garden Curator, Elizabeth Lawrence House & Garden, winghavengardens.org

Liz Rogers, Assistant Head, Curator of Manuscripts, Special Collections, Marriott Library, University of Utah

Janine Biunno, The Isamu Noguchi Foundation and Garden Museum.

Sonia Christon, Bibliothécaire, Musée Rodin.

Sandi West, The Atlanta Journal-Constitution.

Kirk Ryan Brown, Garden Comm, Magnolia Plantation

Joel T. Fry, Curator, Bartram's Gardens.

Library of Congress

Archives.org

ForgottenBooks.com

Gutenberg.com

Quotegarden.com

Wikipedia.com

Wikiquote.com

Libquotes.com

ILLUSTRATIONS

Page 95   Strawberries. Dreer's mid-summer catalogue 1921. Henry A. Dreer (Firm) Henry G. Gilbert Nursery and Seed Trade Catalog Collection. Philadelphia, Pa. Electronic resource.

Page 102   Carque's Fig Advertisement. Walter E. Smith Co. Nov. 12, 1913. History of Soybeans and Soyfoods in France (1665-2015). Soyinfo Center. 2015. Shurtleff, William, Aoyagi; Akiko. Electronic resource.

Page 111   "The White Lily." Thornton, Robert John (circa 1768-1837). - Peter Henderson. London: Aug.1st., 1800. Hand-coloured and colour-printed aquatint engraving by Stadler.

Page 136   Teapot Hedge. Collins-Pittman, Jean, photographer. Scotland. 19, April 2008.

Page 171   Blake, William. *Songs of Experience*. 1794. The Sick Rose. Plate 39. Fitzwilliam Museum. Electronic resource.

Page 179   H.W. Buckbee (Firm) H.W. Buckbee (Firm) Henry G. Gilbert Nursery and Seed Trade Catalog Collection, H.W. Buckbee seed and plant guide 1907. Rockford, Ill. Buckbee. U.S. Department of Agriculture, National Agricultural Library

Page 190   Sanders, Francis – Vicar of Hoylake, and Irvine, William Fergusson. "Wirral Notes and Queries, being local gleanings, historical and antiquarian, relating to the Hundred of Wirral," from many sources. 1893. Wilmer Bros & Co. Birkenhead. Page 107. Electronic resource.

BIBLIOGRAPHY

"Henry V". By William Shakespeare. The Globe Theatre, London. c. 1599. Printed.

"Venereal." Merriam-Webster.com Dictionary, Merriam-Webster, *https://www.merriam-webster.com/dictionary/venereal. Accessed 13 Aug. 2019.* n.d.

Addison, Joseph. *A Letter From Italy*. London: H. Hills, 1709. Electronic.

Addison, Julia De Wolf. *Arts and crafts in the middle ages; a description of mediaeval workmanship in several of the departments of applied art, together with some account of special artisans in the early renaissance* . Boston: L. C. Page & company, 1908. Electronic.

Administrador. *Sermons and Biblical Work*. 18 August 2016. https://www.biblia.work/sermons/carvergeorge-washington/. 2018.

Aken, Olivier Van. *Nature, ScienceAlert* Fiona MacDonald. 31 May 2016. Electronic.

Alger, William Rounseville. "The New Era Volume 2." 1872: p. 315. Electronic.

Allingham, William. *Songs, Ballads, and Stories*. London : G. Bell, 1877. Electronic.

Ammianus. *The Greek Anthology, Volume IV, Book XI: "The Convivial and Satirical Epigrams"*. London, New York: W. Heinemann, G.P. Putnam, 1916-1918. Electrical.

Anglicus, Bartholomaeus. *De Proprietatibus Rerum*. Madgeburg, Saxonia , 1240. Electronic.

Anonymous. *A Book of Fruits and Flowers*. London: M.S. for Thomas Jenner, 1653. Electronic.

Aragorn, Louis. *Paris Peasant*. Paris: Editions Gallimard, 1926. Electronic.

Back to Methuselah (A Metabiological Pentateuch). By George Bernard Shaw. Garrick Theatre, New York City . 27 February 1922. Electronic.

Bacon, Sir Francis. *A collection of apophthegms, new and old*. London: Andrew Cooke, 1674. Electronic.

Bacon, Sir Francis. "Of Gardens." Bacon, Francis. *The Works of Francis Bacon/Volume 1*. New York: R. Worthington, 1884. The Essayes or Counsels, Civills and Moralls, of Francis Lo. Verlum Viscount St. Alban (1625). Electronic.

Baker, Ray Stannard. *Great Possessions: A New Series of Adventures*. Garden City, New York : Doubleday, Page & Company , 1916. Electronic.

Banks, Iain. *Use of Weapons* . London: Orbit UK, 1990. Print.

Bartlett, L. W. "There's Something in Me Like Something in You."

The National Magazine Volume XLVI April 1917 to September 1917.
Electronic.

Bashō, Matsuo. *The Sea and the Honeycomb: A Book of Tiny Poems*.
Boston: Beacon Press, 1971. Printed.

Beck, Hanna Rion Ver. *Let's Make A Flower Garden*. New York:
McBride, Nast, and Company, 1912. Electronic.

Beck, Simone, Louisette Bertholle and Julia Child. *Mastering the Art
of French Cooking*. New York City: Alfred A. Knopf, 1961.
Printed.

Beckett, Samuel. *Watt*. Paris: Olympia Press, 1953. Electronic.

Beecher, Henry Ward. *"Beecher: Christian Philosopher, Pulpit
Orator, Patriot and Philanthropist: A Volume of Representative
Selections from the Sermons, Lectures, Prayers, and Letters of
Henry Ward Beecher"*. New York: Belford, Clarke, & Co,
1888. Electronic.

Bennett, Dan. 2015. Electonic.

Berry, Wendell. *The Art of the Commonplace: The Agrarian Essays*.
Washington, D.C.: Counterpoint, 2002. Electronic.

—. *The Gift of Good Land: Further Essays Cultural and Agricultural*.
Berkeley: Counterpoint, 2009. Print.

—. *The Unsettling of America: Cultur & Agriculture*. Berkeley:
Counterpoint, 2015. Electronic.

Bierce, Ambrose. *The Cynic's Word Book* . London: Arthur F. Bird,
1906. Electronic.

Blackmore, Sir Richard. *The Poetical Works of Sir Richard Blackmore*. Edinburgh: Mundell and Son, Royal Bank Close, 1793. Electronic.

Blake, William. *Songs of Innocence and Experience* . London: W Blake, 1794. Electronic .

Blom, Jinny. *The Thoughtful Gardener*. London: Jacqui Small; Illustrated edition , March 16, 2017. Printed.

Blumen-, Frucht- und Dornenstücke oder Ehestand, Tod und Hochzeit des Armenadvokaten F. St. Siebenkäs im Reichsmarktflecken Kuhschnappel — "Flower, Fruit, and Thorn Pieces; or, the Married Life, Death, and Wedding of the Public Defender F. St. Siebenkäs i. Berlin ; Leipzig ; Frankfurt a.M., 1796 -1797. Electronic.

Bohn, Harry George. *A Handbook of Proverbs*. London: George Bell and Sons, 1855. Electronic.

Boorde, Andrew. *The fyrst boke of the introduction of knowledge or, a dyetary of helth*. London: N. Trubner & Co., 1542, 1870. Electronic.

Bovee, Christian Nevell. *Intuitions and Summaries of Thoughts*. Boston, New York: W. Veazie; Sheldon and company, 1862. Electronic.

Brault, Robert. *Round Up The Usual Suspects Thoughts on Just About Everything*. North Charleston, SC: CreateSpace, 2014. Printed.

Breck, Joseph. *The Flower-Garden, or Breck's Book of Flowers*. Boston: John P. Jewett and Company, 1851. Electronic.

Brown, J. Carter. *Creating the Art of Culture* Academy of
Achievement. 5 May 2001. Electronic.

Browne, William. *Britannia's Pastorals*. London: Geo. Norton, 1613.
Electronic.

Browning, Elizabeth Barrett. *Aurora Leigh*. London: Chapman and
Hall, 1856. Electronic.

—. *Poems Vol II* . London: Chapman and Hall , 1850. Electronic.

—. *Sonnets from the Portuguese and other love poems*. London:
Chapman and Hall , 1850. Electronic.

Bryant, William Cullen. "An Invitation to the Country ." *Harper's
Weekly* May 1857. Electronic.

—. *POEMS: by William Cullen Bryant, An American*. Cambridge,
Massachusetts: Hilliard & Metcalf,, 1821. Electronic.

Bucchianeri, Elizabeth Ann. *Vocation of a Gadfly*. Batalha Publishers,
2018. Electronic.

Bulwer-Lytton, Sir Edward George Earle. *The Poetical and
Dramatical Works of Sir Edward Bulwer-Lytton* . Piccadilly,
London: Chapman and Hall , 1854. Electronic.

Burgess, Thornton. *The Burgess Animal Book for Children*. Boston:
Little, Brown and Company, 1920. Electronic.

Burroughs, John. *Winter Sunshine*. Boston : Houghton, Mifflin. and
Company, 1875. Electronic.

Burton, Hilarie. *Esquire Presents Me in My Place with Hilarie Burton
Esquire*. 6 June 2011. Electronic.

Buxton, Charles. *Notes of Thought*. London: John Murray , 1883. Electronic.

C., C. Joybell. *Vade Mecum*. Scotts Valley: CreateSpace Independent Publishing Platform , 2013. Electronic.

Cable, George Washington. *The Amateur Garden*. New York: C. Scribner's Sons, 1914. Print.

CaliforniaFigs.com . 2013. Electronic. 2015.

Carpenter, Novella. *Farm City: The Education of an Urban Farmer* . London: Penguin Press, 2009. Electronic.

Carver, George Washington. "1897 Or Thereabouts George Washington Carver's Own Brief HIstory of His Life." 1897. *https://www.austintexas.gov/sites/default/files/files/Parks/Carve r_Museum/Carver_Bio_and_Information.pdf*. Electronic. 2015.

Carver, George Washington and edited by Gary R. Kremer. *George Washington Carver: In His Own Words*. Columbia, MO: University of Missouri Press, 1987. Printed.

Carver, George Washington. *The Man Who Talked with the Flowers: The Intimate Life Story of Dr. George Washington Carver*. Saint Paul, Minn: Macalester Park Publishing Co, 1939. Electronic.

Cary, Phoebe. *Poems and Parodies*. Boston: Tickner, Reed, and Fields, 1853. Electronic.

Chanakya and Translated by Miles Davis and V. Badarayana Murthy. *Sri Chanakya Niti-shastra; the Political Ethics of Chanakya*. India: Ram Kumar Press, 1981. Electronic.

Chesterton, G. K. *The Autobiography of G. K. Chesterton*. New York: Sheed & Ward, 1936. Electronic.

Child, Lydia Maria. *Letters from New York*. New York, Boston : Charles Francis and Company, James Munroe & Co., 1843. Electronic.

Christopher, Lucy. *Stolen: A Letter To My Captor*. Frome, United Kingdom: Chicken House, 2009. Printed.

Clouston, William Alexander. *Book of Wise Sayings, Selected Largely from Eastern Sources* . London: Hutchinson & Co, 1893. Electronic.

Collins, Edward James Mortimer. *The British Birds, a communication from the Ghost of Aristophanes*. London: The Publishing Co, 1872. Electronic.

—. *Thoughts in My Garden*. London: Bentley, 1880. Electronic.

Concord, Brook Farm and. *Early Letters of George Wm. Curtis to John S. Dwight*. New York and London: Harper & Brothers, 1898. Electronic.

Cornwall, Barry. *Dramatic Scenes: and other Poems*. London: Ollier, 1819. Electronic.

Cowper, WIlliam. *Adam: A Sacred Drama. Translated from the Italian of Gio. Battista Andreini*. 1810.

Cowper, William and and Charles Ryskamp Ed. John D. Baird . *The Poems of William Cowper. 3 vols. VII*. Oxford: Oxford University Press, 1980. Electronic.

Cowper, William. *Poems: by William Cowper, of the Inner Temple, Esq.* London: Joseph Johnson, 1782. Electronic.

—. *The Task: A Poem, in Six Books.* London: Joseph Johnson, 1785. Electronic.

—. *The Works of William Cowper, Esquire Vol X.* London : Baldwin and Cradock , 1837. Electronic.

Cruso, Thalassa. *The Gardening Year.* New York : Alfred A. Knopf, 1973. Print .

Crusso, Thalasso. *To Everything There Is a Season: The Gardening Year.* New York: Alfred A. Knopf, 1973. Print.

Curtis, George William. *Early Letters of George Wm. Curtis to John S. Dwiight.* New York, London: Harper & Brothers, 1898. Electronic.

—. *Literary and Social Essays of George Wm. Curtis.* New York: Harper & Brothers, 1895. Electronic.

—. *Nile Notes of an Howadji.* New York: Harper & Brothers, 1852. Electronic.

—. *Trumps.* New York: Harper & Brothers, 1861. Electronic.

Dawes, Rufus. *The Valley of the Nashaway and other poems.* Boston: Carter & Hendee, 1830. Electronic.

Delaplaine, Joseph. *Delaplaine's repository of the lives and portraits of distinguished American characters.* Philadelphia, 1815. Electronic.

Dorr, Julia Caroline Ripley. ""Without and WIthin"." *Sonoma Democrat, olume XV, Number 23* 16 March 1872. Electronic.

\

Dryden, John. *Examen Poeticum : Being the Third Part of Miscellany Poems Containing variety of New Translations of the Ancient Poets.* . London: R E For Jacob Tonson, 1693. Electronic .

Dudley, Charles. "My Summer in A Garden." *The Harford Courant* 1870. Electronic.

Dumas, Alexander. *Le Grand Dictionnaire de Cuisine.* Paris: Pierre Grobel, 1873. Electronic.

Dumas, Alexandre. *La Tulipe Noire.* Paris: Baudry, 1850. Electronic.

Eliot, George. *Silas Marner.* Edinburgh and London: William Blackwood and Sons, 1861. Electronic.

—. *The Mill on the Floss.* Edinburgh and London: William Blackwood and Sons, 1860. Electronic.

Emerson, Ralph Waldo. *Early Poems of Ralph Waldo Emerson. Introduction by Nathan Haskell Dole.* . New York, Boston: Thomas Y. Crowell & Company, 1899. Electronic.

—. *Nature; addresses, and lectures.* Boston and Cambridge: James Munroe and Company, 1849. Electronic.

—. *Poems.* Boston: James Munroe and Company, 1847. Electronic.

Erickson, Louis Bernard. "Lou's News." *The Atlanta Constitution, The Atlanta Journal* 5 March 1951 -1982: Editorial Column. Print.

Eryngium of North America. USDA PLANTS. https://plants.usda.gov/core/profile?symbol=ERYNG

Ethel Waters, Charles Samuels. *His Eye Is On The Sparrow.* New York City: Doubleday & Company, 1951. Print.

\

Evelyn, John. *Acetaria, A Discourse on Sallets*. London: B. Tooke,
1699. Electronic.

—. *Directions for the Gardiner and other Horticultural Advice*.
London: Sir Geoffrey Keynes, Oxford University Press, 1666,
1932, 2009. Electronic.

Fforde, Jasper. *Shades of Grey*. London: Hodder and Stoughton, 2009.
Electronic.

Fields, James Thomas. *Ballads and Other Verses*. Boston: Houghton,
Mifflin, and Company, 1880. Electronic.

Finley, Ron. *Guerilla Gardening in South Central LA*. TED2013,
2013.
https://www.ted.com/talks/ron_finley_a_guerrilla_gardener_in_
south_central_la.

Flammarion, Camille. ""Mars, by the Latest Observations"." *Popular
Science Monthy Volume 4* Dec 1873. Electronic.

Florida, History Network. *Florida Stature 15.032*. Tallahassee, 16
April 1967.
https://www.flsenate.gov/Laws/Statutes/2015/15.032.

*Folks, This Ain't Normal: A Farmer's Advice for Happier Hens,
Healthier People, and a Better World*. New York City : Center
Street Hachette Book Group, 2011. Printed.

Forester, C. S. *The African Queen*. New York: Little, Brown and
Company, 1935. Electronic.

Fuller, Thomas. *Gnomologia: adagies and proverbs; wise sentences
and witty sayings, ancient and modern, foreign and British*. London:

B. Barker, A. Bettesworth, C. Hitch, 1732. Electronic.

Gagliano, Dr. Monica. ""Green Symphonies: a call for studies on acoustic communication in plants." ." *Behavioral Ecology, Volume 24, Issue 4* (July-August 2013): 789–796. Electronic.

Garofalo, Michael Peter. *Pulling Onions - #61 http://www.gardendigest.com/laws.htm*. 2017. Electronic.

Gass, William H. *READING RILKE: Reflections on the Problems of Translation* . New York: A. A. Knopf, 1999. Printed.

George Eliot, pseudonym of Mary Ann Evans. *Adam Bede*. Edinburgh and London: William Blackwood and Sons, 1859. Electronic.

Gilbert, William Schwenk. *The Bab Ballads*. London: John Camden Hotten, , 1868. Electronic.

Giono, Jean. *Regain*. Paris: B. Grasset, 1830. Electronic.

Goldsmith, Oliver. *The Captivity an oratorio, Act 1*. London: Wm Pickering, 1764. Elecronic.

Grizzard, Lewis. *Atlanta Journal-Constituton* 1977 - 1989. Electronic.

Gross, Anna Goldmark. *The Gnomes of Saline Mountain*. New York City: The Shakespeare Press, 1912. Electronic.

Gza. *"Science and The Genius"* Mary Carmichael. 3 December 2011. Electronic.

Hall, Donald. *LIfe Work*. Boston: Beacon Press, 1993. Printed.

Hartley, Florence. *The Ladies Book of Etiquette and Manual of Politeness: a complete handbook for the use of the lady in polite society*. Boston: G. W. Cottrell, 1860. Electronic.

Hayley, William, 1745-1820. *Cowper's Milton, in four volumes*. Chichester: W. Mason for J. Johnson & Co, 1810. Electronic.

Heaney, Seamus. *Death of a Naturalist*. London: Faber and Faber, 1966. Electronic.

Hemans, Felicia Dorothea Browne. *The Last Autumn at a Favorite Residence with other poems and recollections*. London: John Murray, 1836. Electronic.

Hemas, Felicia Dorothea Browne. *Poemsn*. London: G. F. Harris, 1808. Electronic.

Hepburn, Audrey. *Audrey Hepburn: An Intimate Portrait* Diana Maycheck. New York Birch Lane Press 1993 . Electronic.

Hertel, Dr. Johannes. *Panchatantra*. Cambridge: Harvard University, 1908. Electronic.

Hiroshi, H. ""On Vis medicatrix naturae and Hippocratic Idea of Physis"." *Memoirs of School of Health Sciences*. Ed. Kanazawa University Faculty of Medicine. http://sciencelinks.jp/j-east/article/199907/000019990799A0162403.php Archived 2008-06-10 at the Wayback Machine., 1998. 22:45-54. Electronic

Hood, John. *The Beauty of God... As Revealed in His Works, His Written Word, and the Living Word Through the Ministry of Life and Light and Love* . Baltimore: J. Lanahan, 1908. Electronic.

Horne, Lena. *People Magazine*. 10 November 1980. www.libquotes.com.

Hoyt, E.W. Co. *Perfumed with Hoyt's German Cologne*. Emergence of
Advertising in America: 1850-1920, 2010.
https://idn.duke.edu/ark:/87924/r4b855b2b.

Hubbard, Alice. ""For Philistines and Roycrofters"." *The Fra:
Exponent of the American Philosophy Vol XI No. 1* August
1913: pages 146-150.

Hunt, Leigh and S. Adams edited by Lee. *The Book of the Sonnet*.
London: Sampson Low, Son, & Marston,, 1867. Electronic.

Hwa, Kim dong. *The Color of Earth*. Korea, New York: First Second,
2003, 2009. Electronic.

ildan, Mehmet Murat. *Murat ildan Quotations*. 2010.
https://ildanmmi6.blogspot.com/.

Irving, Washington. *The Alhambra: a series of tales and sketches of
the Moors and Spaniards* . Philadelphia: Carey & Lea, 1832.
Electronic.

Jacula prudentum, or, Outlandish proverbs, sentences &c. London:
T.M. for T. Garthwait , 1651. Electronic.

Jefferson, Thomas and Edwin Morris Betts. *Thomas Jefferson's
Garden book, 1766-1824 with relevant extracts from his other
writings*. Philadelphia: American Philosophical Society, 1944.
Electronic.

Jefferson, Thomas. "Extract from letter to W. Fleming." 28 November
1809. *Jefferson Quotes & Family Letters*. Electronic. 2015
http://tjrs.monticello.org/letter/1609 RC (IEN). PoC (DLC).

—. "Extract from Letter To William Hamilton." Dft (DLC). July 1806.

Jefferson Quotes and Family Letters. Electronic.

—. "Extract from Thomas Jefferson to Bernard McMahon." 15 July
1806. *Jefferson Quotes and Family Letters*. Electronic.
http://tjrs.monticello.org/letter/1809 RC (IEN). PoC (DLC).
2015.

—. "Extract from Thomas Jefferson to Francis Eppes." (ca. 1786).
Jefferson Quotes and Family Letters. Electronic.
http://tjrs.monticello.org/letter/1645 2015.

. "From Thomas Jefferson to George Washington, 28 June 1793,"."
https://founders.archives.gov/documents/Jefferson/01-26-02-
0360. [Original source: The Papers of Thomas Jefferson, vol.
26, 11 May–31 August 1793, ed. John Cata. *Founders Online,
National Archives*. Electronic. 2015.

—. "Thomas Jefferson to Bernard McMahon, 16 February 1812,"
Founders Online, National Archives,
https://founders.archives.gov/documents/Jefferson/03-04-02-
0388. [Original source: The Papers of Thomas Jefferson,
Retirement Series, vol. 4, 18 June 1811 to 30 Ap." n.d.

Joyce, James. "Ulysses." *The Little Review* (1918 -1920): Chicago.
Electronic .

Kabir. *Songs of Kabir*. 15th century. Electronic.

Keller, Helen. *Midstream My Later Life*. Garden City, New York:
Doubleday, Doran & Company, 1930. Electronic.

—. *The Story of My Life: With Her Letters and a Supplementary
Account of her Education*. New York City: Doubleday, Page &

Company, 1903. Printed.—. *To Love This Life: Quotations by Helen Keller*. Arlington: AFB Publications, 2000. Print.

Landor, Walter Savage. *Pericles and Aspasia Volume 1*. London: Saunders and Otley, 1836. Page 117. Electronic.

—. *The Works of Walter Savage Landor Vol II*. London: Edward Moxon, 1846. Electronic.

Lawrence, David Herbert. "THe Odour of Chrysanthemums." *The English Review* July 1911. Electronic.

Lequenne, Fernand, "Mon Ami le Jardin", Paris, Swquan, 1941. Electronic.

Lisieux, Carmel De. "http://www.archives-carmel-lisieux.fr/english/carmel/index.php/story-of-a-soul-in-the-making-1897-1898." 2015. *Archives Du Carmel De Lisieux.* Electronic.

Lisieux, St. Thérèse of. *Story of a Soul*. Bar-Le-Duc: Imprimerie de L'Oeuvre de Saint Paul , 1898. Electronic.

Locker, Frederick. *London Lyrics*. London: Chapman and Hall, 1857. Electronic.

Longfellow, Henry Wadsworth. *The Children's Longfellow Illustrated* . Boston & NY: Houghton MIfflin Company, 1908. Electronic.

Lowry, Chris, Dr. University of Bristol. "Getting Dirty May Lift Your Mood." ScienceDaily. ScienceDaily, 10 April 2007. <www.sciencedaily.com/releases/2007/04/070402102001.htm>.

MacDonald, Fiona. ":Plants Really Do Respond to The Way We Touch Them, Scientists Reveal."." *Nature, ScienceAlert* 3 May 2016.

Electronic.

—. *Plants Really Do Respond to The Way We Touch Them, Scientists Reveal*. Sydney, Australia, 3 May 2016.

Marvin, Rev. Dwight Edwards. *Curiosities in Proverbs*. New York, London: G. P. Putnam & Sons, 1916. Electronic .

McVeagh, Diana M. *Elgar The Music Maker* . Woodbridge, Suffolk, UK: Boydell Press, 2007. Electronic.

Meigs, Cornelia. *Master Simon's Garden*. New York : The MacMillan Company, 1916. Electronic.

Melville, Lewis. *Beau Brummel, His Life and Letters* . London: Hutchinson, 1924. Electronic.

Meyers, Stephanie. *Twilight*. New York City: Little, Brown and Company, 2005. Printed.

Millay, Edna St. Vincent. *Renascence and Other Poems*. New York City: Harper & Brothers, 1917. Electronic.

—. *Second April* . New York: Mitchell Kennerly , 1921. Electronic.

—. *The Harp-Weaver and The Other Poems*. London and New York: Harper & Brothers, 1923. Electronic.

Milne, A. A. *Not That It Matters* . New York: E.P. Dutton & Co., 1920. Electronic.

MItchell, Henry Clay. *The Essential Earthman: Henry Mitchell on Gardening*. New York City: Houghton Mifflin Harcourt, 1998. Print.

Moore, Thomas. *Lalla Rookh, an Oriental Romance*. London: Thomas Y. Crowell & Company, 1817.

Morton, Kate. *The Forgotten Garden*. Crow's Nest, New South Wales: Allen & Unwin, 2008. Printed.

Moss, Charlotte. "Charlotte Moss's New Textile Collection." *Architectural Digest* December 2011. Electronic.

Muir, John. *A Thousand-Mile Walk To The Gulf*. Boston and New York: Houghton and Mifflin, 1916. Electronic.

Naso, Publius Ovidus. *The Heroïdes, Or Epistles of the Heroines; The Amours; Art of Love and minor works*. Rome, ca. 5 BC. Electronic.

Newell, Peter Sheaf Hersey. *Peter Newell's Pictures and Rhymes*. New York and London : Harper & brothers, 1899. Electronic.

O'Donnell, Rebecca. *Freak: The True Story of an Insecurity Addict* . Bloomington: iUniverse, 2011. Electronic .

O'Keefe, Patrick. "The History of Say It With Flowers." unk. *www.CreativeReview.co.uk* . Electronic. 2017.

O'Keeffe, Georgia. *New York Post* 16 May 1946. Electronic.

Oldfield, Molly and John Mitchinson. "QI." *The Telegraph* 10 September 2012. Electronic.

Oldfield, Molly and John MItchinson. "QI." *The Telegraph* 6 March 2013. Electronic.

Othello. By William Shakespeare. The Globe Theatre, London. 1603. Electronic.

Ouseley, Sir Gore. *'Biographical Notices of Persian Poets, with Critical and Explanatory Remarks'* . London: Oriental Translation Fund of Great Britain and Ireland', 1846. lectronic.

Page, Russell. *The Education of the Gardener*. New York City: Atheneum, 1962. Electronic.

Percival, James Gates. "The Language of Flowers ." Unpublished, 1872. Electronic.

Phillpotts, Eden. *The Book of Avis: A Trilogy Comprising Bred in the Bone, Witch's Cauldron, A Shadow Passes*. London: Hutchinson & Co., 1936. Electronic.

Pizarnik, Alejandra. *The Galloping Hour: French Poems*. New York City: New Directions , 2018. Electronic.

Plutarch. *Parallel Lives of Noble Grecians and Romans*. London: Jacob Tonson, 100 AD, 1727. Electronic.

Poincelot, Achille. *Visiting Hours*. Vancouver: House of Parlance Media, 2005. Print.

Poincelot, Achilles. *Étude de l' Homme ou Reflexions Morales* . Paris : Comon & Co, 1846. Electronic.

Pope, Alexander. *An Essay on Man. In Epistles t a Friend. Epistle II*. London: J. Wilford, 1733. Electronic.

Proust, Marcel. *Sodom et Gomorrhe III. La Prisonnière*. Paris : Gallimard, 1923. Electronic.

Quintinie, Jean de La. *he compleat gard'ner, or, Directions for cultivating and right ordering of fruit-gardens and kitchen-gardens with divers reflections on several parts of husbandry, in six books : to which is added, his treatise of orange-trees, with the raising of melons,*. London: M. Gillyflower, 1693. Electronic.

Rabbit Takes a Holiday/Eey! Eeyi! Eeyore! . Dir. Jamie MItchell, Ken Kessel Terrance Harrison. Perf. Eeyore (Peter Cullen). Sep 29, 1990. Television .

Rappaport, Herbert. *Holiday Blues: Rediscovering The Art of Celebration*. Philadelphia: Running Press, November 7, 2000. Electronic .

Read, Thomas Buchanan. *Poems*. Boston: William Ticknor & Company, 1847. Electronic.

Reichhold, Jane. *Basho: The Complete Haiku*. Tokyo: Kodansha International Ltd., 2008. Electronic.

Richter, Jean Paul Friedrich. *Levana, or The Doctrine of Education*. Braunschweig: Gedruckt und verlegt bei Friedrich Vieweg, 1807. Electronic.

Rikle, Rainer Maria. *Letters of Rainer Maria Rilke*. New York: W.W.Norton And Company Inc., 1945. Electronic.

Rodin, Auguste. *Art*. Boston: Small, Maynad & Company, 1912. Electronic.

Romeo and Juliet . By William Shakespeare. The Globe Theatre, London. 1597. Print .

Romeo and Juliet. By William Shakespeare. The Globe Theatre, London. 1597. Electronic.

Root, Waverley. *Food: An Authoritative, Visual History and Dictonary of the Foods of the World*. New York City: Simon & Schuster, 1986. Printed.

Ruskin, John. *Prosperina: Studies of Wayside Flowers* . New York:

John Wiley & Son, 1875. Electronic .

—. *Sesame and Lilies*. New York: J. Wiley & son, 1865. Electronic
source.

—. *The Stones of Venice*. London: Smith, Elder & Co., 1853.
Electronic.

Sabatini, Rafael. *The Sea Hawk* . London: Martin Secker, 1915.
Electronic.

Saint–Exupéry, Antoine de. *The Little Prince*. New York, Paris:
Reynal & Hitchcock (U.S.), Gallimard, (Fr), 1943. Print.

"Schanpsleiche Spirits." *http://www.schnapsleichespirits.com/home*.
Woodville, WA, 2016.

Schwab, Charles M. *Succeeding with What You Have*. New York: The
Century Co., 1917. Electronic.

Scott, Sir Walter. *Quentin Durward*. Edinburgh, London: Archibald
Constable and Co; Hurst, Robinson, and Co., 1823. Electronic.

—. *The Antiquary*. Edinburgh, London: Archibald Constable;
Longman, Rees, Orme, Brown and Green, 1816. Electronic.

Secundus, Gaius Plinius. *Pliny's Natural History*. Encyclopedia
Britannica, 1911. Electronic.

Shīrāzī, Abū–Muhammad Muslih al–Dīn bin Abdallāh. *The Gulistan*.
Shiraz, Iran: unknown, 1258. Electronic.

Silverstein, Shel. *Where the Sidewalk Ends*. New York City: Harper
and Row, 1974. Printed.

Smith, Eliza. *The Compleat Housewife, or Accomplished
Gentlewoman's Companion*. Philadelphia: J. Pemberton, 1727.

Electronic.

South, Robert. *Sermons Preached Upon Several Occasions Vol V* .
London: J. Bettenham for Jonah Bowyer, 1727. Electronic.

St. John The Good. World Heritage Encyclopedia Edition , 2017.
Electronic

Stegner, Wallace. *Angle of Repose*. New York: Doubleday, 1971.
Print.

—. *On Teaching and Writing Fiction*. New York: Penguin Books,
2002. Electronic.

Stephen, Sir Leslie. *Studies of a Biographeer*. New York, London:
G.P. Putnam's Sons; Duckworth & Co, 1898. Electronic.

Stevenson, Robert Louis. "The Ideal House." *Essays of Travel, 1905*.
London: Chatto and Windus, 1898.

Stewart, Amy. *The Drunken Botanist: The Plants That Create the
World's Great Drinks*. Chapel Hill: Algonquin Books of Chapel
Hill, 2013. Printed.

Stryk, Lucien, "Matsuo Bashō," The American Poetry Review, Vol.
13, No. 2, March/April, 1984, pp. 33-5.

SunWolf, Dr. *https://professorsunwolf.com/words.html*. post 2009.
Electronic. 2017.

Swift, Jonathan. *Gulliver's Travels - Travels into Several Remote
Nations of the World. In Four Parts. By Lemuel Gulliver, First
a Surgeon, and then a Captain of Several Ships*. London:
Benjamin Motte, 28 October 1726. Electronic.

Taylor, Baynard. "Angelo Orders His Dinner." *The Atlantic Monthly* January 1871. Electronic.

—. "Ode on a Jar of Pickles." *The Atlantic Monthly* February 1872. Electronic.

Tennyson, Lord Alfred. *Poems Chiefly Lyrical* . London: Effingham Wilson, Royal Exchange, 1830. Electronic.

Teresa, Mother. *In the Heart of the World: Thoughts, Stories, and Prayers*. San Francisco : New World Library, 1997. Printed.

The Madwoman of Chaillot. By Jean Giraudoux. Théâtre de l'Athénée, Paris. 19 December 1945. Written in 1943. Electronic.

The Sea Hawk . Dir. Michael Curtiz. Perf. Brenda Marshall Errol Flynn. 1940. Television.

Thomas, Dylan. *The Map of Love: Verse and Prose.* J. M. Dent and Sons. London. Publication year: 1939. Page 7.

Thoreau, Henry David. *Journals*. Boston and New York: Houghton Mifflan and Company, 1906. Electronic.

—. *Walden; or, Life in the Woods*. Boston: Ticknor and Fields, 1854. Electronic.

Three Wise Fools. Dir. Edward Buzzell. Perf. Lewis Stone Margaret O'Brien. 1946. Electronic .

Traditional German Proverb. n.d. Electronic.

"Traditional Kurdish Saying." 2014. Electronic.

Tolkien, J. R. (1982). *The Fellowship of the Ring / First part of the Lord of the Rings* (Vol. Chapter 6, p. 328). Boston: Houghton Mifflin.

Troilus and Cressida. By William Shakespeare. The Globe Theatre, London. ca. 1602. Print.

Tse-Tung, Mao. *Socialist Upsurge in the Countryside*. Peking: Foreign Languages Press, 1957. Electronic .

Tuckerman, Henry Theodore. *The Optimist*. New York: George P. Putnam, 1850. Electronic.

Twain, Mark. "Pudd'nhead WIlson's Calendar ." *The Century Magazine* (1893-1894). Electronic.

—. *Roughing It*. Hartford, Conn: American Publishing Company, 1872. Electronic.

Volpone. By Ben Jonson. Globe Theatre, London. 1606. Electronic.

Walton, Izaak. *The Compleat Angler*. London: Thomas Y. Crowell & Company, 1653. Electronic.

Warfield, Catherine Ann and Eleanor Percy Ware Lee. *Wife of Leon and other poems* . New York, Philadelphia: D. Appleton and company, G.S. Appleton , 1844. Electronic .

Warner, Charles Dudley. *My Summer in a Garden*. Boston: James R. Osgood & co, 1870. Electronic.

Weil, Dr. Andrew. ""Why Plants Are (Usually) Better Than Drugs." *The Blog, The Huffington Post* 19 January 2010. Electronic .

Whitney. *"Not Seeing Is A Flower"* . San Diego International Airport . *Window Mural Installation* . San Diego, 2018. Personal.

"Who Started "Say It with Flowers?". *Printer's Ink* 5 Jan 1922: 87. Electronic.

Wilde, Oscar. "The Picture of Dorian Gray." *Lippincott's Monthly Magazine* J. B. Lippincott & Co. July 1890. Electronic.

Wilhelm Tell. By Johann Christoph Friedrich von Schiller. Weimar. 17 March 1804. Electronic.

Woolever, Adam, compiled by. *Treasury of Wisdom, Wit and Humor, Odd Comparisons and Proverbs*. Philadelphia: David Mackay, 1877. Electronic.

Worsley, Lucy. *"Fit To Rule"*. London, 15 April 2013 . BBC News Magazine. Electronic .

Wortabet, John. *Wisdom of the East, Arabian Wisdom Seleections and Translations from the Arabic*. London: John Murray, 1907. Electronic.

Young, Edward. *The Universal Passion*. Dublin: S. Powell, for George Ewing, 1725. Electronic.

AUTHOR INDEX

BOTANICAL INDEX

HASHTAG INDEX

179, 180, 185,
  186, 187, 195,
  197
#essays, 12, 13
#eternity, 83
#etymology, 101
#evolution, 181
#exercise, 27,
  167, 171, 177
#experience, 144
#export, 101
#eyesore, 60

F

#fairies, 36, 72
#fairytales, 80
#faith, 110
#family, 38, 72,
  159
#farm, 96, 103,
  138, 153, 154.
  156
#farmtotable, 94
#fiction, 70, 72,
  159
#fishing, 97, 98
#flattery, 101
#Florida, 105
#florist, 85, 88
#flowers, 44,

116, 175
#food, 108, 135,
  136, 139, 169
#foreign, 11
#forest, 57, 91
#forgetfulness,
  135, 136
#forgiveness, 63
#fragrance, 10,
  47, 48, 153
#frailty, 148
#France, vi, 10
  27, 46, 54, 79,
  82, 100, 104,
  107, 118, 136,
  148, 153, 169,
  181, 196
#friends, 119
#friendship, 26,
  33, 46, 48, 79
#fruit, 13, 15,
  27, 97, 99,
  100, 101, 105,
  109, 110, 116,
  118, 119, 128,
  133, 137, 138,
  139, 173, 188
#funeral, 55

G

#gambling, 175
#genetics, 158
#Germany, 50,
  56, 151, 167
#gifts, 16, 85
#gloves, 148
#gnomes, 36
#God, 17, 78
#gold, 45
#goodness, 16,
  19
#goodwill, 153
#gothic, 70
#gratitude, 146
#GreatBritain,
  72, 180
#Greece, 101,
  119, 166, 172,
  196
#green, 149
#greenhouse, 31,
  32
#grocery, 108,
  138
#growth, 164

H

#haiku, 91, 109
#hands, 151
#happiness, 33
#healing, 162,
  163, 178
#health, v, 145,

CPSIA information can be obtained
at www.ICGtesting.com
Printed in the USA
BVHW061415061221
623342BV00014B/190